Teaching
for the
TWO-SIDED
MIND

Linda VerLee Williams

A Guide to Right Brain/Left Brain

Education

Teaching
for the
TWO-SIDED
MIND

A SPECTRUM BOOK

Prentice-Hall, Inc., Englewood Cliffs, New Jersey 07632

Library of Congress Cataloging in Publication Data

Williams, Linda Verlee.
    Teaching for the two-sided mind.

    "A Spectrum Book."
    Bibliography: p.
    Includes index.
    1. Learning.   2. Thought and thinking.   3. Brain—
Localization of functions.   I. Title.
LB1060.W54 1983   370.15'23   83-4429
ISBN 0-13-892554-2
ISBN 0-13-892547-X (pbk.)

This book is available at a special discount when ordered in
bulk quantities. Contact Prentice-Hall, Inc., General
Publishing Division, Special Sales, Englewood Cliffs, N.J. 07632.

3   4   5   6   7   8   9   10

ISBN 0-13-892554-2

ISBN 0-13-892547-X {PBK.}

Editorial/production supervision by Peter Jordan
Cover design © 1983 by Jeannette Jacobs
Manufacturing buyer: Doreen Cavallo

Prentice-Hall International, Inc., *London*
Prentice-Hall of Australia Pty. Limited, *Sydney*
Prentice-Hall Canada Inc., *Toronto*
Prentice-Hall of India Private Limited, *New Delhi*
Prentice-Hall of Japan, Inc., *Tokyo*
Prentice-Hall of Southeast Asia Pte. Ltd., *Singapore*
Whitehall Books Limited, *Wellington, New Zealand*
Editora Prentice-Hall do Brasil Ltda., *Rio de Janeiro*

To Andy, Erin, and Megan

CONTENTS

Preface *xi*

1

LEARNING WITH
THE WHOLE BRAIN *1*
The Two-Sided Mind and Education

SCIENTIFIC THEORY
AND EDUCATIONAL PRACTICE *13*
Differences Between the Hemispheres
A Model of Specialization
Implications for Education
Learning Styles and the Hemispheres
Teaching Techniques for the Right Hemisphere

HOW DO YOU THINK? *39*
Strategies and Modes of Thinking
Teaching Students Process Awareness
Solutions to Exercises

METAPHOR *54*
Advantages of Metaphorical Teaching
Using Metaphor in the Classroom

VISUAL THINKING *84*
Training Perception
Graphic Representation
Visualization

FANTASY *115*
Experiencing Fantasy
Observation Fantasies
Identification Fantasies
Fantasy as a Basis for Self-Expression
Evaluating the Products of Fantasy
Using Fantasy in the Classroom
Further Applications

MULTISENSORY LEARNING   143

Sensory Learning in the Early Primary Grades
Sensory-Motor Integration
Kinesthetic and Tactile Learning
Kinesthetic Learning in Academic Subjects
Kinesthetic Perception in Physical Learning
Smell and Taste
Nonverbal Auditory Learning (Music)

DIRECT EXPERIENCE   168

Laboratory Experiments
Field Trips
Real Objects and Primary Source Material
Simulation
Role Playing

HOW TO START   180

Planning for Change
Starting Now
Intangibles
Rediscovering Your Subject
Personal Growth
Working Together
Support Groups

10

CONCLUSION *191*

Bibliography *197*

Index *209*

PREFACE

Recent research on the hemispheres of the brain has made us aware that we possess two different and complementary ways of processing information—a linear, step-by-step style that analyzes the parts that make up a pattern (in the left hemisphere) and a spatial, relational style that seeks and constructs patterns (in the right). That discovery has stirred considerable excitement among educators and created a desire to explore the application of hemispheric research to the classroom. This book is an effort to bridge the gap between research and application. It presents the current research on the functioning of the hemispheres, explores the implications of that research for education, and provides practical teaching techniques which draw upon the capabilities associated with the right hemisphere.

I have chosen to focus on techniques which we have reason to connect with the processing style of the right hemisphere, not because they are more important than those associated with the left hemisphere (they are not), but because they are much less well known. We have a good deal of experience with linear, analytical approaches to education. If we are to teach for the full range of students' cognitive abilities, we must *balance* those techniques with others which make use of the right hemisphere's preference for patterns and wholes and its visuo-spatial capacities.

The techniques in this book deal with how material is taught, not what is taught. Therefore, they are applicable to any subject and any grade level. I have included numerous examples of their actual application in classrooms from elementary through high school, in a wide variety of subjects, and with a range of ability levels from gifted to low achievers. The schools from which these examples are drawn represent rural, suburban, and urban settings. Some of the techniques will be new to most teachers; others are used by many teachers already but become much more effective when they are understood and applied within the context of a two-sided approach.

Teachers of students with learning disabilities have shown particular interest in hemispheric research. I have not set aside a section on that subject but have treated specific topics at various points throughout the text. Reports from teachers indicate that for some students the inclusion of more right hemisphere approaches is very helpful. However, the range of problems that are lumped together as learning disabilities is so great that there are no approaches that work equally well with all students.

Because I work primarily with teachers in the schools, I have addressed this book to them. However, the book should be equally useful for students in training to become teachers. In fact, new teachers have a great advantage in that they can adopt a two-sided approach without having to modify an established teaching style. In addition, I hope that some parents and older students may find the book useful. The information in chapters 1–3 should be of interest to anyone curious about the brain and learning, and the techniques presented in chapters 4–8 can serve as learning strategies as well as teaching techniques.

To use a new technique, one must have some personal experience with it. Therefore, whenever possible, I have included exercises which readers can do to experience the techniques for themselves. For those using the book as part of a course, discussion of these exercises should also provide insight into differences in personal learning and teaching styles.

Finally, there is a personal dimension hidden beneath the

objective language of this book. In 1970 when I began the work that led to *Teaching for the Two-Sided Mind,* I was a very linear, verbal thinker. I could not visualize an apple, I had never experienced the conscious use of relaxation or fantasy, and I was woefully unaware of my body. Discovering that there were areas of my life that I'd relinquished by not using them, I decided to reclaim them. I made a conscious effort to visualize and draw, to search for metaphors, to develop the parts of myself I'd neglected. I did not give up being a linear, verbal thinker and I did not become an artist. But I've become confident enough of my visual abilities to design (not to draw) the mandala on page 3 (Figure 1.1) and to tackle and enjoy a number of projects I would have avoided twelve years ago.

The point of this story is that right hemisphere techniques are accessible to anyone, and that if you claim them and use them, they become yours. They enrich not only your teaching but your life because they open new possibilities and allow new growth. All you need is the willingness to try something new, something you may not be good at immediately.

One of the nice things about being a teacher is that everything you learn about yourself is useful in your work and much that you learn at work can be food for your own growth. I hope the ideas in this book will nourish both.

It would be difficult to acknowledge individually all the people who contributed to this book by their ideas, help, and examples. I owe special thanks to William J.J. Gordon, Tony Poze, Robert McKim, David Straus, Victoria Sperry, Hildred Yost, Jeannine Herron, and Marsha Beck for introducing me to many of the concepts and techniques in the book and for reading and commenting on the chapters related to their work. My thanks also to Frank Doran, Ron Jones, Jim Kerr, Herbert Kohl, and George Leonard for expanding my definition of what education can and should be. Any errors that remain despite this excellent help are, of course, my own.

In the area of graphics, I wish to thank Elly Simmons for the mandala used as Figure 1.1, Jane Rockwell for drawing Figures 1.3, 2.3, 3.2, 3.3, and 5.1, Marjorie Garlin for Figure 2.1, Gene

Davis and Alex Grishaver for the cartoons used for Figures 5.6 and 5.7, and Maureen Chambers for the mandala in Figure 5.5. My thanks also to Genie Miller and Mary Frances Claggett who generously shared with me art work done by their students.

A great many teachers have helped to shape my thinking. Some are acknowledged in the text; others are not, but I owe much to all of them. I would also like to thank the teachers and others who've read and commented on sections of the book: Sharon Boren, Mary Frances Claggett, Lynn Crook, Gene Davis, Jim Grass, Peter Hanawald, Sara Hennen, Sheila Kogan, Gail Kohlhagen, Judi Magarian-Gold, Sonia Martin, Genie Miller, Afriye Quamina, Barbara Semenoff, and Becky Wheat. My special thanks to Phyllis Koppelman and Mary Dwan who provided much appreciated editorial and moral support, to Ruth Bernard for inspiration and sanctuary; to Elizabeth Fischel, Jeremy Joan Hewes, Mollie Katzen, and Carolly Erickson for laughter and comfort; and most of all to my husband, Andy, for his support, encouragement, and gentle but honest editing.

LEARNING WITH
THE WHOLE BRAIN

In the last fifteen years research on the brain has exploded as new techniques allow scientists to probe areas previously restricted to the realm of speculation. No research has stimulated more interest than that on the two halves of the brain, for in revealing that the hemispheres function differently, it suggests that we expand our concept of intellectual processes. Our current definition of thinking has tended to emphasize verbal, analytical processes. We now have proof that this view ignores half of the mind's capabilities. What of the other half? What new possibilities open to us if we expand our approach to teaching to take advantage of both hemispheres?

To answer that question we must understand the types of processing used by the two hemispheres (Chapter 2 will provide a much more thorough discussion of this subject). The left hemisphere is sometimes described as *analytical* because it specializes in recognizing the parts that make up a whole. This discussion is an example of analysis; it takes apart left-hemisphere processing and describes it in terms of the functions it performs. Left-hemisphere processing is also *linear* and *sequential;* it moves from one

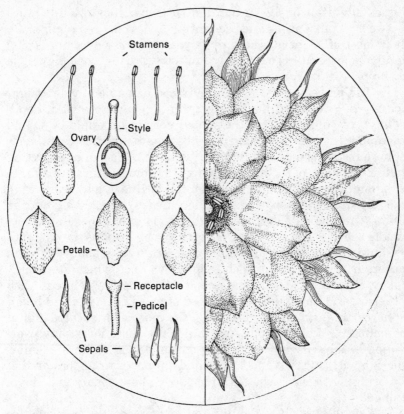

Figure 1.1   We possess a single brain, but it is made up of two hemispheres which process information in very different ways. Chapters 1 and 2 will describe those differences in words; Figure 1.1 presents them in the form of an image. Before you proceed to the words, take a moment to study the image and consider the differences it suggests.

point to the next in a step-by-step manner. It is most efficient for processing verbal information, for encoding and decoding speech.

While the left hemisphere is busy separating out the parts that constitute a whole, the right specializes in combining those parts to create a whole; it is engaged in *synthesis.* It seeks and constructs patterns and recognizes relationships between separate parts. The right hemisphere does not move linearly but processes simultaneously, in parallel (to experience the difference between simultaneous and sequential processing, see Figure 1.2). It is most efficient at *visual and spatial processing* (images). Its language capacity is extremely limited; words seem to play little or no part in its functioning.

The preceding discussion is a good example of what might loosely be called left-hemisphere thinking. A more right-hemisphere way of presenting the same information would be to find metaphors for the hemispheres—that is, to describe each hemisphere in terms of something that is like it. We can compare the left hemisphere of the brain to a digital computer and the right to a kaleidoscope. The digital computer is linear and sequential, moving from one step to the next by rules of logic and a language of its own. The kaleidoscope simultaneously combines its parts to create a rich variety of patterns. It moves by leaps as the parts are reshuffled and reassembled in different relationships to each other. In the computer each step determines which steps may follow it, while in the kaleidoscope the parts may relate to each other in an almost infinite number of ways. The cerebral hemispheres are far more complex than the most sophisticated digital computer or kaleidoscope, but while the metaphors may oversimplify, they also give us a way of connecting unfamiliar information with our own experience and enhance our understanding by bringing together the features of each hemisphere in a single image.

Our discussion of the differences between the hemispheres should not obscure the fact that it is their *complementary* functioning that gives the mind its power and flexibility. We do not

Figure 1.2 To experience the difference between *sequential* and *simultaneous* processing, look at the two sets of series and find the item that does not belong in the series. Did you do this task by moving your eyes from left to right checking each item in order until you found the one that didn't fit? Then you used sequential processing. Or did you look at the whole line and let your eyes focus on the item that broke the pattern? That's simultaneous processing.

A   B   C   D   E   F   C   G   H   I   J   K

0   *   0   *   0   0   *   0   *   0   *   0

think with one hemisphere or the other; both are involved in higher cognitive processes. Figures 1.1 and 1.3 demonstrate the advantage of processing information both verbally and visually. Imagine how the chart in Figure 1.3 would be if it consisted only of words or of pictures. In either case it would convey less information. Look again at Figure 1.1. Notice how in a single image it represents the difference between part and whole, verbal and visual, linear and patterned. Together, words and images communicate more clearly than either could alone.

The power of the two-sided mind is demonstrated most dramatically in accounts of creative discoveries. Any significant creative breakthrough is usually preceded by a good deal of primarily logical, linear thinking as an individual defines and redefines a problem. Then there comes a moment of insight when an answer presents itself, and finally the mind tackles the difficult job of evaluating the insight and putting it into a form in which it can be communicated and applied to the problem. Ask scientists or inventors, and they can tell you of the logical, analytical work that precedes and follows the insight, but they are often vague on the subject of how they arrived at the insight. In one

Figure 1.3 The differences between the processing styles of the left and right hemispheres represented both verbally and visually.

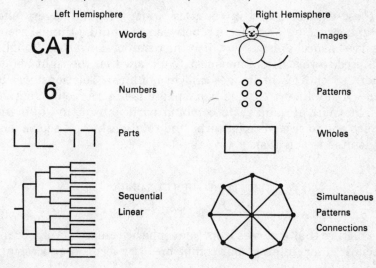

account after another, you read of answers "coming to" individuals; and the manner in which insights and discoveries "come" is never logical. Here are two examples:

> The chemist Kekule came upon one of the most important discoveries of organic chemistry, the structure of the benzene ring, in a dream. Having pondered the problem for some time, he turned his chair to the fire and fell asleep: "Again the atoms were gamboling before my eyes. . . . My mental eye . . . could now distinguish larger structures . . . all twining and twisting in snake-like motion. But look! What was that? One of the snakes had seized hold of its own tail, and the form whirled mockingly before my eyes. As if by a flash of lightning I awoke." The spontaneous inner image of the snake biting its own tail suggested to Kekule that organic compounds, such as benzene, are not open structures but closed rings.[1]
> Charles Duryea was an engineer who had been struggling with the apparently unsolvable problem of how to develop an efficient system for introducing fuel into the engine of an automobile. One day in 1891 he observed his wife at her dressing table spraying herself with her perfume atomizer. Although Duryea knew about the function and existence of perfume atomizers, he had not made a connection until that moment; but now he saw at once how to build the spray-injection carburetor.[2]

In these examples and in countless others, inner imagery and metaphor (seeing a connection between two unlike things) seem to serve as mechanisms by which the result of nonverbal thought is offered to verbal consciousness. We know that the right hemisphere specializes in images and in nonlinear relationships. It seems likely then that this hemisphere is the source of creative insight. With its ability to combine parts into many different wholes and to recognize patterns and relationships, it seems ideally suited to this task.

THE TWO-SIDED MIND
AND EDUCATION

The picture that emerges from hemispheric research is of a brain specialized for different but complementary forms of processing.

One form is not superior to the other; effective thinking requires both. Given the importance of these two types of thinking, one would assume that both would be included in our education system. Unfortunately, this is often not the case. The brain has two hemispheres but too often the education system operates as though there were only one.

In the typical high school classroom, students are expected to learn most of their information from books and lectures. They work almost exclusively with words and numbers, in a world of symbols and abstraction. Even in elementary school, mimeographed sheets and workbooks increasingly replace the direct experience which allows young students to learn with all their senses. In such classrooms, one hemisphere gets a lot of use, the other very little. Students who are less proficient at verbal processes are required to learn in a manner that is unnecessarily difficult for them and are thus unable to function at their full potential. Their more verbal classmates may *appear* to be learning very well, but they are getting little or no help in developing and using right-hemisphere thinking. Since these processes are essential to problem solving and creativity, their omission is a serious loss.

Making fuller use of the two-sided mind does not require giving up books and lectures. They are valuable teaching techniques. It merely requires that we balance them with other techniques more appropriate to the right hemisphere. Instead of beginning a unit on chemical bonding by assigning a chapter in the textbook, then discussing the material in class, giving review questions, reviewing, and finally administering a multiple-choice or essay test, a teacher might begin with a fantasy that shrinks students to the size of an atom and takes them on an exciting journey through the world of atoms and molecules. The teacher could guide them into several common substances—water, air, or salt, for example—describing what they'd see, hear, and feel. After the fantasy they might draw the molecules as they'd experienced them. These drawings would tell the teacher where confusion existed and make it possible to correct any misconceptions. The textbook reading could then be assigned with a greater likelihood that students would be interested and would understand it. With their corrected drawings before them, the students could discuss the reading. The teacher's lecture would be supplemented by as many pictures as possible as well as by drawings and diagrams on the board so that students could see as well as hear the information. To review and help students integrate their learning, the teacher could set up a problem-solving exercise using balls of clay or Styrofoam and colored toothpicks. Students could construct different types of atoms and put together simple molecules. The test could allow students to demonstrate understanding with drawings or diagrams as well as with words.

A two-sided unit requires more of the teacher because it uses some new techniques, but it also gives a great deal more to the student. By presenting information in a number of ways, it allows each student to learn in the way that is most efficient for that individual, and it also exposes the student to different ways of learning and develops a variety of thinking skills. The first time it's taught, such a unit requires more preparation time, but it need not take longer to teach than the traditional unit. In fact, because comprehension and motivation are improved, the teacher spends less time reviewing and repeating and has more time for activities which are stimulating and enjoyable.

The power of right-hemisphere techniques in teaching is demonstrated by the experience of Diane Streeter, an English teacher from Serramonte High School in Daly City, California. Ms. Streeter was assigned to teach eleventh graders an elective class in grammar, that most linear and verbal of subjects. By the middle of the semester all who had mastered the material had been assigned to independent study, and she was left with many students who had studied grammar for a number of years and still couldn't identify parts of speech or analyze sentences. She decided to use fantasy with them. The students were asked to close their eyes and imagine that they were nouns. Afterward they discussed their fantasies; most reported feeling heavy, boxy, immobile. Fantasies with verbs and other parts of speech followed. In other exercises they imagined relationships between different parts of speech, derived symbols, and translated sentences from symbols and vice versa. By the end of the unit the majority of the students had mastered parts of speech and could manipulate those elements in simpler forms of sentence construction. They were so confident in their abilities that some asked if they could be tested with the "smart" students. The "failures" generally equaled and in some cases surpassed their "smart" classmates. The right-hemisphere technique of fantasy had enabled them to succeed in learning a subject they'd been unable to master through a more linear, analytical approach. Interestingly enough, many of the students who had succeeded at learning grammar by traditional methods had difficulty generating fantasies. Because they'd never been asked to use their imaginative faculty in school, this deficiency had gone unnoticed. While their grades did not reflect it, they suffered from a disability as severe as that of their less analytical classmates.

For Ms. Streeter's "failures" and students like them who are not primarily verbal in their approach to the world, inclusion of right-hemisphere techniques can mean the difference between success and failure. These students are currently being expected to work in ways that are at odds with their learning style; it is not unlike demanding that they function in a foreign language when they have only a minimal grasp of it. We will be much more effective if we teach to their strengths.

Students like Ms. Streeter's "smarts" who are successful with verbal, linear processes suffer a hidden deficit. Without encouragement to develop their right-hemisphere capabilities, they come to rely on a limited number of strategies and are at a disadvantage in situations which require a full range of intellectual abilities. Patricia Davidson, whose work on math styles will be discussed in Chapter 2, offers an example of how this hidden deficit operates. She points out that often students who are successful in written computation in the early grades are not encouraged to use manipulative materials that develop spatial thinking. Many of these students have great difficulty later when they encounter more advanced forms of math that require spatial and conceptual thinking.[8] This situation where apparent success paves the way for later failure is one cost of emphasizing a single type of processing at the expense of its complement.

The research on the brain supports what many teachers have intuitively known, that students learn in many ways and that the more ways one can present information, the better they will learn. When lessons are presented visually as well as verbally, when students make their own connections between what is to be learned and what they already understand, and when all the senses are engaged in the learning process, students are able not only to learn in the way best suited to their style, but also to develop a full and varied repertoire of thinking strategies. The purpose of this book is to suggest the practical techniques teachers can use to broaden their approaches to a subject to include both left- and right-hemisphere thinking. These techniques need not be added on; they do not require that time be taken from something already in the curriculum. They deal with *how* material is taught, not *what*. For most subjects, important concepts are presented at least four times; they are introduced, explained, reviewed, and tested. If each of those steps utilizes a different approach to learning, students can use a full range of thinking styles to understand the subject. Learners will be able to use their individual strengths to master the material while at the same time developing the skills in which they are deficient.

While this book presents techniques that teachers can use with a minimum of equipment, it is important to recognize that microcomputers, which are becoming increasingly common in schools, also offer exciting possibilities for stimulating right-hemisphere learning. Computers, like human teachers, have the potential to stimulate students to think in a variety of ways. The drill and practice programs often associated with computer-assisted instruction demand a largely linear, left-hemisphere processing style. But there are many other programs and ways of using computers which stimulate relatively greater right-hemisphere thinking. An understanding of the differences between the left and right hemispheres can be applied to evaluating computer programs and should help you select those which develop both types of thinking.

In the next chapter we'll review the research on the cerebral hemispheres and suggest a model of how they function. We'll also identify and discuss teaching techniques which draw on the strengths of the right hemisphere. Chapter 3 contains a series of exercises to help you discover more about your own thinking style. Chapters 4 through 8 are devoted to the right-hemisphere techniques—metaphor; visual thinking; fantasy; kinesthetic, musical, and multisensory learning; and forms of direct experience. These chapters are highly practical; their goal is to provide tools teachers and students can use in the classroom. Chapter 9 offers practical suggestions for teachers who want to start making right-hemisphere techniques a more important part of their teaching repertoire. The final chapter summarizes the main points of the book and provides the opportunity to extend and share your own efforts at right-hemisphere teaching. This book is designed to give you some experience with each of the techniques, enough guidance to begin using them in your classroom, and practical suggestions for making both short- and long-range changes in your teaching style.

It is difficult to do the two-sided mind justice in the linear, verbal presentation of a book. Doing is part of knowing, and for this reason exercises are included wherever possible to enable you to experience directly the processes and techniques being discussed. Take the time to do the exercises. They will help you discover ways in which the information is personally relevant and will give you additional insight into the material being presented.

Many teachers report that one outgrowth of their exploration of right-hemisphere teaching is an expansion of their own capacities and interests. What begins as an effort to teach more effectively becomes a personal quest to develop long-neglected abilities within themselves. Metaphor, fantasy, visual and multisensory thinking, and kinesthetic perception are not just teaching techniques—they are basic powers of the mind. As you work to develop them in your students, you will find them becoming an increasingly potent part of your own mental tool kit, and you will discover applications that go far beyond this book.

NOTES

1. From R. H. McKim, *Experiences in Visual Thinking* (Monterey, Calif.: Brooks/Cole, 1972), p. 9, by permission of the publisher. Copyright © 1972 by Wadsworth Publishing Co.

2. WILLIAM J. J. GORDON and TONY POZE, *The New Art of the Possible* (Cambridge, Mass.: Porpoise Books, 1980), p. 7.

3. LORRAINE LOVIGLIO, "Mathematics and the Brain: A Tale of Two Hemispheres," *The Massachusetts Teacher* (January–February 1981), pp. 13–14.

SCIENTIFIC THEORY
AND EDUCATIONAL
PRACTICE

Interest in the operations of the human mind probably goes back to the dawn of human consciousness, for it is the mind more than any other faculty that distinguishes us from the other animals with whom we share the planet. The ancient Greeks located the mind in the heart rather than the brain. They believed that since the mind was essential to humanness, it must be the most vital of all organs. Knowing that wounds to the head were often but not always fatal while wounds to the heart were always deadly, they reasoned that the mind must be located in the heart. Science eventually corrected that misconception, but further knowledge of the functions of the brain came slowly, and it is only in recent years that we have developed the techniques to begin to unravel the mysteries of the brain.

If we look at the brain from above, we see that it is divided into two equal and seemingly identical parts, rather like a walnut (see Figure 2.1). For scientists those two parts, the right and left cerebral hemispheres, have long been the subject of study and debate. In the nineteenth century, lacking the more sophisticated devices we possess today, scientists assumed the hemispheres to

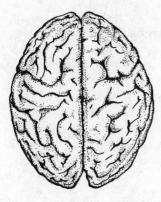

Figure 2.1
The human brain as seen from above.

be identical and wondered whether nature had provided a second, duplicate hemisphere as "backup" in case of injury to the primary hemisphere. In 1865 Paul Broca reported that injuries to a certain area of the left cerebrum almost invariably produced speech disorders while injuries to the same area of the right hemisphere did not. Nine years later in Germany Carl Wernicke identified another region outside Broca's area associated with a different type of speech impairment and again found that language was affected only by injury to the left hemisphere. In both cases, the researchers determined that the disability did not involve the muscles producing speech but that each area was involved in a basic mental process required for production of meaningful spoken language.

It seemed clear that if lesions in the left hemisphere affected language while those in the right did not, the hemispheres were not identical. Given the importance Western culture places on verbal processes, it is not surprising that scientists assumed the left hemisphere to be not just different from but superior to the right; and the theory of hemispheric dominance was born. This theory seemed to be supported by the fact that in the majority of people the right hand (controlled by the left hemisphere) is dominant.[1] Since little was known of the right hemisphere, it was dismissed as not playing a significant role in thinking.

However, study of patients with damage to the right hemisphere seemed to contradict this assumption. World War II pro-

15

vided researchers with a large sample of brain-injured patients, and their investigations revealed that right-hemisphere lesions produced difficulty in a number of important areas. While patients with damage to the right hemisphere retained their verbal abilities, they often experienced extreme spatial distortion; many had great difficulty finding their way around the ward, getting lost on their way to the bathroom or being unable to find the mess hall. They had difficulty dressing themselves—often putting clothes on upside down or with a limb in the wrong hole. Their drawings also revealed severe problems with spatial relations, demonstrating great disorganization and distortion of relationships between various elements.

Researchers discovered that many of these patients responded differently to familiar and unfamiliar shapes. They theorized that familiar shapes could be labeled and were thus handled by the verbal left hemisphere; however, patterns which were unfamiliar and not easily labeled relied on the right hemisphere for processing. The right hemisphere was superior at guessing what a whole figure might be when only a part of it was revealed. It was also better at making discriminations between colors. In fact, whenever a task required fine or subtle pattern discrimination, the right hemisphere assumed the dominant role. This was true not just for the visual realm but for the other senses as well. Patients with right-hemisphere damage had difficulty discriminating which of two pressures on the body was sharper or exactly where they'd been jabbed by a pin (tactile discrimination). They also had problems learning mazes when blindfolded.[2] The picture which emerged from these studies was that the right hemisphere specialized in visuo-spatial functions, in pattern perception, and in discrimination of fine and subtle patterns in all sensory modalities.

Studies of brain-damaged patients required considerable time and a large sample of patients; therefore, there was great excitement in the early 1960s when a team of surgeons led by Roger Sperry at the California Institute of Technology performed a series of operations which made it possible to study the two hemispheres in isolation from each other. Sperry's work was of such import that he was awarded a Nobel prize for it in 1981. He was working with patients severely afflicted with epilepsy. Earlier experiments with cats had shown that one could separate the brain hemispheres by cutting the corpus callosum, the thick bundle of fibers that connects the two hemispheres and allows them to be in constant communication with each other. Sperry believed that by cutting the corpus callosum in his patients he could prevent the epileptic seizure from spreading from one hemisphere to the other. Thus, though the seizure occurred, it would be isolated in a single hemisphere, and the patient would still have a second, unaffected hemisphere to maintain normal function. These split-brain patients effectively possess two brains within one body. Information transmitted to only one hemisphere cannot be transferred to the other and remains in the receiving hemisphere alone.

A commissurotomy—the cutting of the corpus callosum—is a radical operation. The corpus callosum is made up of approximately 200 million nerve fibers. This number is greater than all the nerve pathways in the spinal cord. The sheer number of fibers should suggest that the integration of the two hemispheres is a complex and highly important function in the brain. One might well expect the destruction of so many nerve fibers to alter significantly the behavior of an individual. However, the split-brain people function fairly normally. It was only through a series of subtle experiments that Roger Sperry and his associates were able to gain insight into the specialization of the two hemispheres.

In most of their daily experiences, the lack of communication between hemispheres does not affect the split-brain patients because both hemispheres receive the same information. However, when researchers manipulate the presentation of information so that it reaches a single hemisphere, they can explore the differences in the functioning of the two sides of the brain. For the first time they can study the functioning of one hemisphere isolated from the other.

Before studying the research one should be aware that the left side of the body is mainly controlled by the right cerebral hemisphere, and the right side is mainly controlled by the left hemisphere; thus stimuli from the right hand, leg, and ear are processed primarily in the left hemisphere and vice versa. The eyes are controlled in a slightly more complex manner. The visual field—that is, what you see—is split so that each eye sends information to both hemispheres. The left half of visual space is seen by the right hemisphere while the right half is perceived by the left hemisphere.

DIFFERENCES BETWEEN THE HEMISPHERES

Verbal vs Spatial.   In one experiment, a split-brain subject was given an object in his right hand when his hands were hidden from sight. He was able to describe and name it. If, however, an object was placed in his left hand, he could do neither. It appeared that he did not know what was in his hand. However, if he was shown an array of objects including the one he'd held and told to pick with his left hand the one he'd had before, he was able to do so, though he was still unable to explain what he was doing. It was clear that he knew what was in his left hand, yet was unable to name or describe it.

The results of this experiment support the model of hemispheric functioning suggested by studies of brain-damaged patients. The right hand communicates with the verbal left hemisphere; thus the subject can describe its contents verbally. The left hand communicates with the right hemisphere; since its verbal capacity is severely limited, the subject cannot provide a verbal answer. However, the lack of a verbal answer does not indicate a lack of knowledge but merely *an inability to express* that knowledge in a verbal form. This experiment has important implications for educators since, in school, knowing is often equated with being able to express oneself verbally.

The right hemisphere is not totally without verbal abilities. If the word *spoon* is flashed to the left visual field, thus the right hemisphere (RH), the subject will not report seeing the word. The left hand (RH) will, however, find a spoon and pick it up from a selection of objects hidden from sight. When asked what the left hand (RH) is holding, the subject will respond, "I don't know."

The right hemisphere, while capable of recognizing the word *spoon* and finding an actual spoon, still cannot describe its functioning in words.

Most right-handers write and draw best with the right hand but have some ability to do these tasks with the left hand, though not so well. After split-brain surgery, the right hand (LH) continues to be able to write but suffers a drastic reduction in its ability to draw. Asked to draw simple figures like a square or cube, it may draw instead a series of angles stacked up but not connected. It seems to be unable to put the parts into their correct spatial relationship. The left hand (RH), not surprisingly, loses its ability to write words correctly. However, it continues to be able to draw. It possesses the spatial, relational sense required for visual representation.[3]

Parts vs Whole Patterns. The right hand's attempts to draw (see Figure 2.2) illustrate another interesting characteristic of the left hemisphere. The overall spatial configuration is missing, but the parts are there. The patients seem to know that the figure is made up of lines and angles but are unable to assemble them to make a figure. They abstract the *parts* but cannot make the *whole.*

Figure 2.2   These drawings of a Greek cross were done by two commissurotomy patients. Notice that in A's right-handed effort, several of the parts of the cross are present, but they are not assembled into the complete pattern. In B's right-handed drawing, the right half of the cross is correctly drawn, but the pattern degenerates into a series of angles (the parts of the cross drawn without a sense of how they fit together to make a whole). The small hand-written numbers beside B's figures indicate which line was drawn first, which second, and so on. (From Joseph E. Bogen, "The Other Side of the Brain I: Dysgraphia and Dyscopia Following Cerebral Commissurotomy," *Bulletin of the Los Angeles Neurological Society*, 34, no. 2 (April 1969), pp. 83 and 91.)

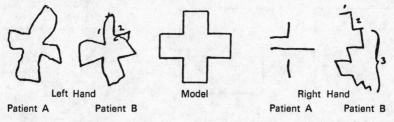

Left Hand   Model   Right Hand

Patient A   Patient B   Patient A   Patient B

Research with brain-injured patients shows the same pattern when they are asked to assemble block designs to match a given model. Figure 2.3 is an example of the difference between patterns constructed by two patients—one with injury to the left hemisphere and the other with damage to the right. The patient with left-hemisphere damage (relying on his relatively intact right hemisphere) maintains the overall configuration of the square (2 × 2, 3 × 3 matrix) but makes an error in the feature on the right side of the figure. The patient with right-hemisphere lesions (obliged to rely on the left hemisphere) loses the overall configuration of the square. He preserves the feature of the lower central point and places it at the center of the square. From these and other tests like them, neuropsychologists have determined that the left hemisphere is specialized to detect features, to reduce a whole to its component parts. The right hemisphere integrates information and perceives patterns, organizing the component parts into a whole. It is important to note that the evidence from both split-brain and brain-injured patients indicates that in order to perform visuo-spatial tasks successfully, an individual relies on the contributions of both hemispheres.[4]

Studies on Normal Subjects. One problem with studies of both brain-damaged and split-brain individuals is that in both cases the brain is abnormal to some degree, and one must consider the

Figure 2.3 Patients' drawings reproduced by permission from Edith Kaplan, from a presentation at the Symposium on Hemispheric Specialization, University of California, University Extension, Berkeley, Calif., October 1980. Original figure in the center reproduced from the Block Design of the Wechsler Adult Intelligence Scale. Copyright © 1955 by The Psychological Corporation. All rights reserved.

  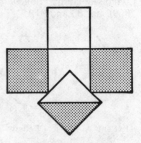

possibility that the findings of studies of these two groups may not apply to normal brains. Fortunately, researchers have developed several techniques which can be used with normal individuals and which seem to confirm the findings of the split-brain research.

One method uses a machine called a *tachistoscope* or specially designed glasses to present stimuli to a single visual field. The tachistoscope can present a stimulus so fast that the subject's eyes can't shift focus. The stimulus thus can only be perceived in a single visual field and is sent to only one hemisphere. In a normal individual the information will be transferred from one hemisphere to the other; however, that transfer will take a few extra milliseconds. It is assumed that if information is sent to the hemisphere where it is processed, the response time will be less than if it's sent to the inappropriate hemisphere and must be transferred. Therefore, by measuring the percentage of correct answers and the time required to do a task or answer a question, the experimenter can tell whether or not transfer took place and thus which hemisphere performed the task.

A second technique relies on a procedure called *dichotic listening*. Subjects are fitted with headphones through which each ear hears a simultaneous, competing stimulus; for example, the left ear (RH) might hear the word *apple* while the right (LH) hears *orange*. The subject is asked what word or stimulus was heard, and the answer tells the experimenter which ear, and thus which hemisphere, had the advantage for processing that stimulus.

Verbal vs Configurational. In experiments using tachistoscopes or dichotic listening, normal subjects are more accurate and faster in recognizing faces, patterns of stimuli, and complex or unfamiliar shapes when they're presented to the left visual field and thus are sent first to the right hemisphere. Melodies, sonar signals, and environmental sounds are also better perceived when presented to the left ear (RH). When verbal stimuli are used, the advantage shifts to the left hemisphere, and subjects perform more accurately with information presented to the right visual field and ear (LH).[5]

In another response time experiment, normal subjects were quicker in identifying as the same, letters that were identical—for example, *A, A*—when they were presented to the left visual field (RH). When letters with the same name but different shapes—for example, *A, a*—were presented, the correct response came more quickly from the right visual field (LH). These results indicate a difference in the way the hemispheres process visually presented verbal material. The left hemisphere seems to use an internal acoustic code; it *names* each letter. The right hemisphere compares the *shapes* of the letters.[6]

This name–shape dichotomy can also be seen in split-brain subjects. When asked to select a picture of an object which is similar to the object in a picture, the two hemispheres use different criteria for their choices. The left hemisphere tends to select an object that is similar in function while the right will choose something that is like the object in its structure or appearance; thus, shown a cake on a plate, the left hemisphere might match it to a knife and fork while the right might select a straw hat (see Figure 2.4). The hat has no logical connection to the cake on the plate, but it is similar in shape.[7]

Serial vs Simultaneous Processing.   It is believed that the two hemispheres differ in the way they process visual stimuli, with the left hemisphere using *serial processing* (one item at a time) and the right operating simultaneously through the use of *parallel* or *holistic processing*. The technique for determining which

Figure 2.4   (From Jerre Levy and Colwyn Trevarthen, "Metacontrol of Hemispheric Function in Human Split-Brain Patients," *Journal of Experimental Psychology: Human Perception and Performance,* 2, no. 3 (August 1976), p. 302. Copyright © 1976 by the American Psychological Association. Reprinted by permission of the author.)

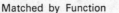

Matched by Function   Matched by Appearance

type of processing is being used is to present the subject with a visual search task (similar to Figure 1.2) and measure the time required to make a decision as the number of items is increased. If the time increases with the addition of more items, the subject is using serial processing; if the time remains the same regardless of the number of items, parallel processing is in operation. Experiments with normal subjects have shown that when they are shown a group of letters and asked to determine whether all the letters are the same, items in the right visual field (LH) are processed serially while those in the left visual field (RH) are processed in parallel.[8]

The existence of different forms of processing is what one might expect given the different demands of processing visuospatial and verbal stimuli. It is clearly to one's advantage to be able to process simultaneously the great amount and variety of information provided by the senses. Using serial processing would result in a reduction of mental efficiency as the number of stimuli increased, a clear disadvantage. For example, if the senses are flooding the mind with stimuli that indicate the approach of a large, predatory animal, any reduction in the speed of processing will have serious consequences. Simultaneous processing has a clear advantage over serial processing in such situations.

Language, however, requires a serial process. Speech sounds are generated in sequence. The meaning of *pat* is different from *tap,* and to distinguish that difference one must be aware of the sounds occurring in a certain order. The process of decoding the acoustic cues of speech is a highly complex operation; the sounds are not neatly separated like the letters of written speech. For example, when one hears the word *big,* information about the first consonant, /b/, may be sent over the first two-thirds of the acoustic signal, information about the vowel may spread over the entire signal, and information about the final consonant, /g/, may occur in the last two-thirds of the signal.[9]

Researchers at Haskins Laboratories are working on the hypothesis that the form of processing of the left hemisphere is specialized for the drastic restructuring required to decode language. They hypothesized that, since some sounds require extensive decoding and others require relatively little, the right ear would show an advantage with sounds that required greater decoding, reflecting greater use of the left hemisphere. They used the fact that stop consonants (such as /b/, /d/, /g/, /p/, /t/, and /k/) require a great deal of decoding while vowels, especially in isolation, demand much less. Dichotic listening experiments demonstrated their hypothesis to be correct. The stop consonants followed by the vowel /a/ did produce a right-ear (LH) advantage while the vowels alone did not.[10]

Language in the Right Hemisphere.   While speech and phonetic analysis appear to be restricted to the left hemisphere, the right hemisphere has greater linguistic abilities than earlier researchers assumed. It can recognize a substantial number of written words and understands an even larger number of spoken words. It does not decode words by a phonetic analysis of the sounds but appears to recognize them by their spatial (sight) or acoustic (listening) patterns. "Sounding out" a word is beyond the right hemisphere; it seems to work directly from the pattern to the meaning. Because it relies on general acoustic cues, the right hemisphere is much less able to distinguish speech from background noise than is the left.[11]

The right hemisphere's ability to perceive patterns enables it to play a unique role in language comprehension. It identifies the intonational contours which distinguish declarative, imperative, conditional, and interrogative sentences in English.[12] At the same time the left hemisphere is not limited to language functions. It engages in a number of processes which have no verbal component; most of these are temporal or time-related in nature. It determines which of two stimuli came first and whether or not stimuli are simultaneous.[13]

In the excitement that followed the early split-brain studies, an oversimplified view of hemispheric functioning emerged. All sorts of dichotomies were ascribed to the two hemispheres—art and science, reason and intuition, cognition and emotion. While scientists have gone far beyond this view, it persists in the general public and, unfortunately, among some teachers. As educators, we cannot afford to oversimplify our view of the brain. Incorrect assumptions can lead to ineffective teaching strategies and inaccurate assessment of students' learning problems.

It is also important to recognize that statements which are true *in general* may not apply to a specific individual. Every human brain is as unique as a fingerprint; no two are exactly alike. Therefore, it is reasonable to assume that no two brains function identically. We know that the brains of left-handed individuals are frequently organized differently from those of right-handers; there is some evidence that differences may exist between the brains of males and females. We do *not* know what, if any, significance to attach to these differences. A classroom is full of individuals; an understanding of how the hemispheres function *in general* should not dull a teacher's sensitivity to each student's uniqueness.

At this point we are working with a model of brain functioning that may well change as we learn more. A model does not represent absolute truth; it is a way of ordering information and explaining new bits of data. In addition, the model presented in this book deals only with the two cerebral hemispheres. The cortex is composed of a number of different regions that are involved in different functions, and it is only part of the brain. Subcortical structures are also involved in learning. A full understanding of the brain must include all of its regions and the relationships between them.

A MODEL
OF SPECIALIZATION

With these qualifications, let's look at the differences which seem to exist between the hemispheres. We will categorize these differences in terms of the type of processing each hemisphere appears to do. The left hemisphere processes *sequentially,* in a step-by-step manner. This linear processing is *temporal* or *time-related* in that it recognizes that one stimulus comes before another. *Verbal* perception and generation depend on the awareness of the order or sequence in which sounds occur. Sequence is important not only in decoding acoustic cues into words but in understanding syntax as well, since the meaning of a series of words depends largely on the order in which they occur. This type of processing relies on the ability to *discriminate the relevant features,* to *reduce a whole to meaningful parts*—in short, to *analyze.*

The right hemisphere appears to specialize in *simultaneous processing* or *processing in parallel.* It does not move from one feature to another but instead *seeks patterns* and *gestalts.* It *integrates component parts* and *organizes them into a whole.* It is interested in *relationships.* This method of processing is most efficient for the majority of *visual and spatial* tasks and for recognizing *musical melodies,* since these tasks require that the mind construct a sense of the whole by perceiving a pattern in visual or auditory stimuli.

Left-Hemisphere Processing	*Right-Hemisphere Processing*
Interested in component parts—detects features	Interested in wholes and gestalts—integrates component parts and organizes them into a whole
Analytical	Relational, constructional, pattern seeking
Sequential processing, serial processing	Simultaneous processing, processing in parallel
Temporal	Spatial
Verbal—encoding and decoding speech, mathematics, musical notation	Visuo-spatial, musical

The primary difference between the hemispheres has been characterized in a number of ways by different researchers. The model presented here assumes that it is the different style of processing of the two hemispheres that influences the functions they perform. Language should not be considered to be "in" the left hemisphere; rather, the processing style of the left hemisphere is the most efficient one to use when dealing with a temporally organized function like language. Similarly, visuospatial thinking is not "in" the right hemisphere. The right half-brain specializes in a mode of processing that perceives and constructs patterns; it is therefore more efficient at visuospatial tasks. The relationship between process and processing style is not immutable; where one of the hemispheres is missing or seriously deficient, it may be more efficient to process *all* skills by the more intact systems.[14] There are no right- or left-hemisphere subjects. Math involves the use of symbols and is often associated with the left hemisphere, but Patricia Davidson of Boston State College has shown that there are *two* major math styles, one that is primarily sequential and the other that relies more on pattern recognition. (Her work will be discussed in greater detail on pp. 29–30.)

The perception of music offers an interesting example of how the brain operates. There is some evidence that it is not the stimulus—the music—that determines where it will be processed but the listener's approach to the stimulus. Listeners who are relatively unsophisticated in music will show a left-ear (RH) advantage, but those who are quite sophisticated are likely to show a right-ear (LH) advantage. We can hypothesize that the naïve listeners respond to the overall contours of the music, to its gestalt, while the sophisticated listeners are processing the same sounds sequentially in a more analytical manner.[15]

IMPLICATIONS
FOR EDUCATION

Hemispheric specialization has significance for all areas of education. Researchers probing the differences in the functioning of the hemispheres are contributing to the understanding of how learning occurs and the factors that create learning problems. Specialists in learning disabilities are drawing on this research to improve techniques for assessing causes of specific problems and suggesting strategies to remediate them. While the work of both these groups will benefit teachers, at present the major application of hemispheric research in the classroom is as a stimulus to reevaluate the teaching techniques we use in light of the new information about how the brain operates.

Researchers in neuropsychology are studying children with

dyslexia and other disabilities to learn how their brains function differently from "normal" students'. Their work may someday provide us with both a better understanding of the nature of learning disabilities and techniques for recognizing and evaluating them. The University of California at San Francisco study of dyslexia did extensive testing of a group of ten- to twelve-year-old dyslexic boys and a control group. While evaluation of their data is not complete, they have found that in their group of thirty-four, twelve subjects could be recognized as dyslexic by one experiment using visual stimuli, while another twelve could be distinguished by a test using auditory stimuli. Only three subjects were included in both groups, suggesting that they suffered from both types of problems. The other thirteen subjects were not distinguished by either the visual or the auditory test. This research suggests that there are at least three types of dyslexia and thus that no single remedial approach will work with all dyslexic students.[16]

In the area of assessing learning disabilities and proposing remedial strategies, the research offers on one hand exciting possibilities for advances and on the other a danger that it will be misused. As research on the hemispheres becomes more widely known, there is a real danger that teachers and resource specialists may assume neurological impairment when they lack adequate means to reach such a determination. Our current tests assess deficits; they do not reveal causes. If teachers assume a child has neurological impairment or "reads with his right hemisphere," they are likely to overlook evidence that does not support their assumptions. A much safer approach is to use the research on hemispheric functioning to assess possible remedial approaches and materials. If a verbal, sequential approach isn't working, one may consider trying a spatial, pattern-seeking strategy, not because one assumes impairment but because this approach offers an alternative which may be more congenial to the child's learning style.

While it is clear that higher mental functions are not localized in the brain, the research gives us a good basis for distinguishing two different types of processing which seem to be associated with the two hemispheres. It indicates that the verbal, analytical process usually identified with thinking is only *one* way of processing information and that a second, equally powerful way also exists. That insight should alert us to the need to broaden our teaching strategies so that we can develop techniques which present and manipulate information in new ways. We can analyze how children go about learning specific subjects or skills in order to discover approaches that seem related to differences in hemispheric processing styles. We can also derive general teaching techniques that are more appropriate to the right hemisphere's processing style and use them to balance our current heavily verbal orientation.

LEARNING STYLES
AND THE HEMISPHERES

Patricia Davidson of Boston State College has studied learning styles in mathematics. Her work is useful not only for math teachers but as an example of how neuropsychological research can be applied to teaching. Dr. Davidson has identified two "math styles." Individuals who depend on Learning Style I

> prefer . . . a "recipe" approach to math, in which they follow a step-by-step sequence of operations, moving forward to a solution. They seldom estimate, tend to remember parts rather than wholes, and have a strong need for talking themselves through procedures. . . . they are often very precise in carrying it [the recipe] out, but while they may arrive at the right answer, they may remain totally unaware of the logic that gives meaning to what they are doing.
> The second general style of math learner . . . is impatient with step-by-step procedures and likely to make mistakes while doing them. Such children are good at estimating, may spontaneously give a correct answer without knowing how it was arrived at, and are superior at recognizing large-scale patterns.[17]

Dr. Davidson has devised diagnostic techniques to assess children's learning styles in math[18] and has designed teaching strategies to build on each child's strengths. Knowing where a child is likely to encounter difficulty, a teacher can help the child develop strategies to deal with those problems. For example, Style I learners can be taught to make the first step of their sequence estimating the answer and the last step checking the actual answer against their estimate. They can be encouraged to talk their way through difficult problems. Style II learners can be taught to use their superior spatial ability and to recognize their own trouble spots and pay particular attention to them.

Dr. Davidson also suggests that teachers tailor the presentation of material to reach students with both learning styles. Problems should be done on the board so that students can see them, and at the same time the teacher should "talk through" the process so students hear it. Often a problem should be done two different ways; to avoid confusion teachers should explain what they're doing and inform students that they need not master both approaches, only the one that's easiest for them.[19]

TEACHING TECHNIQUES FOR THE RIGHT HEMISPHERE

At the same time that we study children's approaches to learning, we can examine specific techniques and general approaches in terms of the types of thinking they require. If all children are to have the maximum opportunity to learn, linear, sequential techniques must be paired with approaches that enable students to see patterns, make use of visual and spatial thinking, and deal with the whole as well as the parts.

Visual Thinking.   One way to accomplish this goal is to balance verbal techniques with *visual strategies*. Words, sentences, and paragraphs are not always the most efficient ways to represent thinking. Many ideas are better expressed and more easily understood through pictures, maps, diagrams, charts, and mind maps. These visual strategies provide images which draw together and integrate information in a form that some students find much easier to understand and remember. They also offer students and teachers an additional way to express and explore ideas.

M. C. Wittrock of the UCLA Graduate School of Education has experimented with the effect of combining verbal and visual activities, and his work demonstrates that the two together are superior to a purely verbal approach. In one experiment, kindergarten and primary school children were taught kinetic molecular theory using pictures, concrete examples, and a simple verbal text. They were introduced to the concepts of molecules in motion, states of matter, and changes in states of matter. The verbal abstractions were all represented graphically and with concrete examples familiar to the children. With this approach two-thirds of the children in one study learned the concepts and remembered them a year later. Their achievement is particularly impressive when one realizes that "these concepts were previously thought to be too complicated for children below Piaget's symbolic (age eleven) or concrete (age seven) levels of intellectual development."[20]

In another study Wittrock demonstrated that students recalled vocabulary words better when they read the definitions and drew their own pictures to represent them than when they read and wrote the words and the definitions. Tracing a picture of the definition produced better recall than writing the definition, but creating one's own visual image was more effective than tracing.[21]

The ability to generate and manipulate visual images is a skill frequently ignored in school, yet there is no reason to assume that thinking which utilizes images is any less efficient or sophisticated than its verbal complement. In fact, Albert Einstein made the following statement:

> The words or the language, as they are written and spoken, do not seem to play any role in my mechanism of thought. The psychical entities which seem to serve as elements in thought are certain signs and more or less clear images which can be voluntarily reproduced and combined. . . . The above mentioned elements are, in my case, of visual and some of muscular type. Conventional words or other signs have to be sought for laboriously in a secondary stage, when the above mentioned associative play is sufficiently established and can be reproduced at will.[22]

For some tasks visualization is by far the most effective strategy for solving the problem; students who have difficulty in this area are at a distinct disadvantage in such situations. For students who tend to be quite verbal, the encouragement of visual thinking in the classroom is essential to the development of that ability. For highly visual students, success in learning academic subjects may depend on their teachers' willingness to allow them to use their primary mode.

Fantasy.   Another form of visual thinking which is relevant to education is *fantasy,* the ability to generate and manipulate mental imagery. As a teaching technique, it can be used to translate verbally presented material into images, making that information more accessible and comprehensible to students. It is also a way of giving students access to their rich store of right-hemisphere images, enhancing the quality of their creative work. Guided fantasy is particularly useful for phenomena one cannot experience first-hand; for example, a textbook analysis of osmosis is too abstract and technical for some students to master. A fantasy in which students imagine themselves either as a membrane or as a molecule passing through a membrane creates inner imagery which is useful to visual thinkers and provides concrete experience that has the power to stimulate and involve many thinkers who are less responsive to a textbook approach.

Evocative Language.   One should not be too quick to dismiss all verbal approaches when considering right-hemisphere teaching. The great difference between the precise language of scientific definition and the rich associative imagery of poetry may reflect a difference in the lexical organization of the hemispheres. There is "some evidence that RH vocabulary is characteristically connotative and associative, and that the LH vocabulary is more precise and denotative."[23] These two types of language may be characterized as *objective* and *evocative.*

Objective language has as its goal precision of meaning; it is the language of definition which prizes clarity and abhors ambiguity. When two scientists are discussing their conclusions, it is essential that they know they both assign *exactly* the same meaning to the words they use. Evocative language, on the other hand, is rich in associations, highly sensual, and much less precise. When Robert Burns writes, "My love is like a red, red rose," he is not concerned with the exact color or qualities of his rose. He uses his words to evoke an image and a set of associations which will be slightly different for each listener. Such language often cultivates ambiguity, suggesting rather than stating, and working on the listener's subjective experience.

An understanding of the two types of language is important for teachers because each type plays a powerful role in learning. In each discipline there are basic concepts which students must learn and terms whose precise meaning it is important to understand, but evocative language also has its place in school. Think, for a moment, of lectures you've attended. You will probably find that the lecturers who made the deepest impression were those who made effective use of evocative language. They were able to make a subject "come alive." Such people often have the ability to create an intense inner experience through their words.

Metaphor.   Another technique which places specific parts within the context of a meaningful whole is *metaphor*. Metaphorical or analogical thinking is the process of recognizing a connection between two seemingly unrelated things. It does not proceed linearly but leaps across categories and classifications to discover new relationships. (It appears that these connections are probably made by the silent right hemisphere and transmitted to the left through some form of imagery.[24]) A car engine and a human body are very different, yet in some ways the car's fuel pump functions like a heart. An understanding of the similarities and differences between the fuel pump and the heart can contribute to the understanding of both mechanisms.

Many teachers introduce the study of electricity by comparing it to water flowing through pipes. They use the metaphor of water in pipes to make a connection between something the students know and with which they're familiar and something which is new to them. When students are asked to generate their own metaphors—for example, to think of something they know that's like electricity—they're challenged to use relational thinking as well as analytical thinking to extend their understanding.

While metaphor does not create experience, it provides the mechanism for establishing a connection between new concepts and previous experience. No new learning occurs in a vacuum; we learn something new by discovering how it relates to what we already know, and the clearer the connection, the easier and more thorough the learning. Metaphors are a mechanism for forging connections.

Direct Experience.   Experiential learning is another way of satisfying the right hemisphere's preference for patterns and whole gestalts. Textbooks present information in a linear manner that emphasizes specific facts and concepts, leaving students with a fragmented rather than an integrated sense of the subject. *Direct experience,* on the other hand, presents students with an opportunity to approach the subject more holistically. They can encounter it with all their senses, getting a "feel" for the whole before trying to master specific pieces of information.

It is sometimes argued that experiential learning takes too much time in comparison to textbook-lecture learning, but there is good reason to question whether the two forms of learning are comparable. Direct experience may be a particularly important way of learning for students who have difficulty with verbal encoding processes because it allows them to use the strengths of their individual learning styles. They can interact with the phenomena they're studying by using their senses to gather and manipulate information nonverbally before facing the task of translating it into the verbal medium. They are not handicapped by the negative reactions which failure experiences from the past may have attached to verbal activities, and because they're being allowed to encounter and engage the material to be learned on their own terms, their motivation and excitement are usually much higher.

Direct experience can take many forms in the classroom. *Laboratory experiments* are one of the most common examples. *Field trips* are another. Whenever possible classrooms should be stocked with *materials that can be manipulated by students—*

Cuisinaire rods, models, collections of objects, and so on. *Primary source material* and *real objects* help enliven subjects like history and social studies with concrete experience. These "real things" provide a kind of learning that supplements and complements verbal approaches. Experience can be created in a classroom through *simulation* and *role playing*. These techniques enable the teacher to set up a situation in which students use and extend their understanding of a subject through an experience which they help to create.

Multisensory Learning. While both hemispheres process sensory stimuli, it seems likely that stimuli that are nonverbal are processed primarily in the right hemisphere. The role of the senses is another area that has been slighted because of our tendency to equate thinking with verbal processes. Yet both the sensory and motor systems play a role in learning, especially in the early years. In addition to the auditory and visual senses, the *tactile and kinesthetic (movement) senses* take in information and help in remembering it. They provide an additional "channel" through which one can reach students who have problems with verbal learning. They are also the primary mode for learning movement skills involved not only in physical education but in subjects like typing and sewing.

Music. While music can be processed in either hemisphere, most listeners seem to use their right hemispheres, so we will include music as a "right-hemisphere technique." Of special interest in this area is the work of Georgi Lozanov, a Bulgarian who uses music to facilitate and accelerate learning of foreign languages. His techniques are being applied to other subjects as well.

In summary, the techniques we've identified as associated with right-hemisphere functioning are not localized in that hemisphere. They do, however, represent ways of processing information which we have reason to connect to the right hemisphere. These techniques are

Visual Thinking
Fantasy

Evocative Language
Metaphor
Direct Experience
   Laboratory experiments
   Field trips
   Manipulation of materials
   Primary sources and real objects
   Simulation
   Role playing
Multisensory Learning
Music

The list, like the verbal, analytical thinking which helped produce it, focuses our attention on discrete entities, obscuring the patterns which connect those entities. Manipulation and fantasy are not separate from visual thinking; visual and kinesthetic perception and imagery are an important part of both techniques. Metaphors are often suggested by direct experience and express themselves to verbal consciousness in the form of visual and other sensory images. The thread which connects all the techniques is that they provide students with an alternative to the verbal, analytical approach which dominates so many classrooms. They allow students to use their full range of intellectual abilities, learning in the way most appropriate to their own thinking style and discovering and developing capacities they might otherwise overlook. The techniques are not intended to replace more traditional verbal techniques; their purpose is to complement them so that the instructional program, like the integrated brain, can make use of a full range of skills and talents.

NOTES

1. Left-handers present interesting questions for researchers. Many have the same brain organization as right-handers; however, some have language lateralized to the right hemisphere, and some have it represented in both hemispheres. Estimates of the percentages of left-handers with each of

these three forms of organization vary, partially because researchers have used different criteria for determining left-handedness. Nevertheless, it is clear that for many left-handers, the brain is organized differently than it is for right-handers. For this reason, statements made about hemispheric specialization apply to right-handed individuals and *some but not all* left-handers.

2. HOWARD GARDINER, *The Shattered Mind* (New York: Knopf, 1975), pp. 356–57.

3. JOSEPH E. BOGEN, "The Other Side of the Brain I: Dysgraphia and Dyscopia Following Cerebral Commissurotomy," *Bulletin of the Los Angeles Neurological Society,* 34, no. 2 (April 1969).

4. EDITH KAPLAN, from a presentation at the Symposium on Hemispheric Specialization, University of California Extension, Berkeley, Calif., October 1980.

5. ROBERT D. NEBES, "Man's So-Called Minor Hemisphere," in *The Human Brain,* ed. M. C. Wittrock (Englewood Cliffs, N.J.: Prentice-Hall, 1977), p. 101.

6. Ibid., pp. 103–4.

7. Ibid., p. 104.

8. Ibid., p. 103.

9. STEPHEN D. KRASHEN, "The Left-Hemisphere," in *The Human Brain,* ed. M. C. Wittrock (Englewood Cliffs, N.J.: Prentice Hall, 1977), p. 111.

10. Ibid., p. 112.

11. ERAN ZAIDEL, "The Split and Half Brains as Models of Congenital Language Disability," in *The Neurological Bases of Language Disorders in Children: Methods and Directions for Research,* eds. Christy L. Ludlow and Mary Ellen Doran-Quine (Washington, D.C.: National Institute of Neurological and Communicative Disorders and Stroke, U. S. Department of Health, Education and Welfare, 1979), p. 69.

12. KRASHEN, "The Left Hemisphere," p. 114.

13. Ibid., p. 115.

14. From JANE HOLMES, "Normal Neuropsychological Development: The Natural History of Learning," a lecture presented at the Symposium on Developmental Neuropsychology, Cal-

ifornia Association for Neurologically Handicapped Children—An Association for Children and Adults with Learning Disabilities (CANHC-ACLD), San Francisco, Calif., January 1982.

15. T. BEVER and R. CHIARELLO, "Cerebral Dominance in Musicians and Non-musicians," *Science,* 185, no. 4150 (August 1974), pp. 537–39.

16. From JENNINE HERRON, "Latest Research News about the Dyslexic Brain," 1981 State Conference of CANHC-ACLD on Learning Disabilities, Los Angeles, Calif., November 1981.

17. LORRAINE LOVIGLIO, "Mathematics and the Brain: A Tale of Two Hemispheres," *The Massachusetts Teacher* (January–February 1981), p. 12.

18. PATRICIA DAVIDSON and MARIA MAROLDA, *Mathematics Diagnostic/Prescriptive Inventory* (MDPI). The MDPI had not yet been published at the time this book went to press but should be available soon.

19. From PATRICIA S. DAVIDSON, "Exploring the Neuropsychology of Math," a workshop presented by CANHC-ACLD, San Francisco, Calif., February 1982.

20. M. C. WITTROCK, "The Generative Processes of Memory," in *The Human Brain,* ed. M. C. Wittrock (Englewood Cliffs, N.J.: Prentice-Hall, 1977), p. 171.

21. Ibid., pp. 171–72.

22. ALBERT EINSTEIN, quoted in J. Hadamard, *The Psychology of Invention in the Mathematical Field* (Princeton, N.J.: Princeton University Press, 1949).

23. ZAIDEL, "The Split and Half Brains," p. 69.

24. WILLIAM J. J. GORDON and TONY POZE, *The New Art of the Possible* (Cambridge, Mass.: Porpoise Books, 1980), pp. 18–19.

HOW DO
YOU THINK?

Chapter 2 provided a left-hemisphere discussion of thinking. Now we'll approach the subject in another way, through direct experience. This chapter will give you an opportunity to explore your own thinking style and to consider how it affects you as a learner and as a teacher.

Most of us know a good deal more about *what* we think than *how* we think, perhaps because so much of our education concerned itself with *what* rather than *how*. We tend to assume that everyone thinks in the same way and that some people are simply better at it than others. In reality, we do not all think the same way at all. We each have our own thinking style. Some people visualize easily and clearly; others have difficulty generating a clear visual image. Linear, analytical thinking is easy for some people, difficult for others.

On the next few pages you'll find a set of problems which you can use to learn about your problem-solving style. There are several ways you can use this series of exercises. One is to do the problems by yourself and study how you've done them. The discussion which follows each exercise will give you some idea of the range of approaches used by different people. Another way to use the problems is to do them with a group of friends or colleagues and discuss together how each of you did each problem. Doing the exercises with a group is an excellent way to learn about thinking styles from adults who are probably more articulate and self-aware than many of your students. It is also a good chance to practice using problems to stimulate a discussion of thinking. If your students are old enough to do the problems, once you've done the exercises yourself you can use them with your class.

You'll find that the following discussion does not refer to right- and left-hemisphere processes. An understanding of the processing styles of the two hemispheres is extremely useful in considering approaches to teaching and learning, but in analyzing how *individuals* learn and solve problems, identifying specific strategies and learning styles offers a more flexible approach. Clearly, certain strategies make relatively greater use of the processing style of one or the other hemisphere, but in studying an individual's approach to problem solving or learning, it is more useful to know what strategies are used well and which are avoided than to speculate on hemispheric involvement. Since the purpose of this chapter is to give you a greater understanding of your own thinking style and to help you do the same for your students, the emphasis will be on strategies and modes of thinking. In chapters 4 through 8, where we will examine approaches to teaching, we will make greater use of the model of hemispheric specialization.

As you do the problems, please try to be aware of *how* you're trying to solve them. What are you doing? Which strategies work and which ones don't? What do you do when an approach doesn't work? Also be aware of how you feel about each problem. Which do you avoid or strongly dislike? Which do you feel confident about? Be aware of which problems are hardest for you and which are easiest. It may be useful to write down a few words to help you remember the steps you went through in solving each problem and approximately how long it took to solve. If you're working with a group, discuss each problem as the group finishes it. If you're alone, read the discussion of each problem after you complete it.

Doing the problems is an important part of learning about

your problem-solving style. However, if you choose not to do them, please do not skip the discussion of each problem because that section contains important information. The solutions to the problems appear at the end of the chapter.

EXERCISE 1

A man and a woman are standing side by side with their weight on their right feet. They begin walking so that each steps out on his or her left foot. The woman takes three steps for each two steps of the man. How many steps does the man take before their right feet simultaneously reach the ground?[1]

There are several ways to approach this problem. Many people *visualize* the two walkers. Some people get such strong imagery that they even experience sounds and smells (a multisensory image); others get a much less distinct picture and must struggle to control the image. Some individuals see *abstract* visual imagery. They see the footprints of the walkers. Such approaches all rely on the strategy of *visualization;* with a problem like this one they are all likely to be effective.

People who have difficulty controlling visual imagery can still use a visual strategy with this problem. They can *draw* or *diagram* the configuration the walkers' feet would make (see Figure 3.3 at the end of this chapter). If you did this, you were probably successful in solving the problem, though it may have taken you a bit longer than it would a person who visualized the situation.

Did you think to use your fingers to *simulate* the walkers, or did you get someone else to walk with you? Both techniques use the body to help solve the problem (a *kinesthetic approach*). Although both are excellent techniques for solving the problem, they are often overlooked because many people have been conditioned not to use their hands and bodies in mental tasks. This cultural bias is extremely unfortunate since it deprives many of us of a valuable tool. The problem can also be solved *mathematically* though the solution is likely to take longer and require more work than if one uses visualization or simulation.

Did you use a *verbal* approach, talking to yourself about the problem? Verbal problem solving is heavily emphasized in school, but it probably did not result in a solution here. This problem is not one for which verbal strategies are usually effective, yet many of us are so conditioned by schooling to approach all problems verbally that it is often difficult for a highly verbal problem solver to give up that approach even when it isn't working.

How did you go about doing the exercise? Did you use a single strategy or did you try several? Many problem solvers limit themselves unnecessarily by getting stuck with the first approach they try; others leap around among strategies too quickly, not taking the time to give any one strategy an honest chance. It's difficult to become conscious of strategic decisions since most of us work fairly automatically, but with practice one can make choices consciously and pragmatically instead of trusting to patterns of functioning laid down long ago. In identifying what strategies you used, don't lose sight of the ones you didn't use. Did you neglect a strategy because it didn't occur to you, because you didn't need it, or because you felt insecure about it?

EXERCISE 2

A painted wooden cube such as a child's block is cut into twenty-seven equal pieces. First the saw takes two parallel and vertical cuts through the cube, dividing it into equal thirds; then it takes two additional vertical cuts at 90 degrees to the first ones, dividing the cube into equal ninths. Finally, it takes two parallel and horizontal cuts through the cube, dividing it into twenty-seven cubes. How many of these small cubes are painted on three sides? On two sides? On one side? How many cubes are unpainted?[2]

How did you solve the problem? Did you use *visualization,* creating and manipulating a mental image of the block? If not, take a minute to try to visualize the cube. Start with the uncut painted cube and imagine making each of the cuts. If you are able to do the problem this way, you are a fairly accomplished visual thinker. If not, don't be discouraged; visual thinking can be improved with practice. As with Exercise 1, you can resort to *draw-*

ing a picture of the problem and solving it that way. Drawing is easier for many people since it does not require holding and manipulating a mental image. The problem can also be solved *mathematically*. Highly *kinesthetic* thinkers might imagine their bodies as the block and feel it divided into twenty-seven pieces. The approach which is least likely to lead to a solution is a *verbal* one.

EXERCISE 3

A large piece of paper, the thickness of this page, is folded once, making two layers. It is folded again, making four layers. If you continue to fold it over upon itself fifty times, how thick is the fifty-times folded paper?[3]

If you tried visualizing this problem, you found that there is a limit to how much one can visualize. Visualizing fifty folds accurately is practically impossible. Once visualization wouldn't work, what other strategies did you try? If you tried to draw the solution, the numbers probably defeated you. If you tried to use a verbal approach, it was no more likely to be successful. The best approach to this problem is mathematical. However, so many people in our society suffer from math blocks that large numbers of people avoid or give up on any problem which they perceive as requiring mathematics. Since an increasing number of situations in our society require at least some knowledge of mathematics, such individuals limit their opportunities to participate and succeed in many areas. Studies indicate that one of the reasons for the concentration of women in certain fields and the shortage of them in others is the fact that so many girls enter college with a poor math background and avoid or are excluded from the math courses which are prerequisite for scientific and technical majors.[4]

EXERCISE 4

Twelve sticks are arranged so that they form three squares. Rearrange the sticks to make eight squares.

Figure 3.1

Did you try to visualize this problem or draw it? Or did you find four sticks (matchsticks, toothpicks, pencils) and move them around to find a solution? If you tried to do the problem in your head or by drawing the sticks, you made it harder for yourself than necessary. The problem involves simple shapes, easily available; yet many people do not think of manipulating objects as a problem-solving strategy. In school, younger students are allowed to handle and manipulate objects as part of the learning process, but as they progress in school, thinking becomes increasingly identified with the head and not the hands. If you didn't work with sticks or matches, find some and try your hand at the problem. Be aware of how it feels to do the problem this way. Are you carrying on an internal dialogue (verbalizing)? There's nothing wrong with that. In fact, it may help you solve the problem, though it's not likely to be sufficient by itself. Be aware of the interaction of manipulation and other strategies.

EXERCISE 5

In this problem only one statement is true. Determine from the information given who did it:
A said, "B did it."
B said, "D did it."
C said, "I did not do it."
D said, "B lied when he said I did it."

Here's a problem where visualization and math are not likely to help you. This problem is more easily solved verbally. One approach is to begin by assuming that A is guilty and determine if in that case only one statement is true; then to assume B to be guilty, and so forth. This method is apt to take a while, but it will yield a solution. A second approach is to notice that since only one statement is true and C says that he didn't do it, one need only discover that A, B, or D is telling the truth to establish that C is guilty (if A, B, or D is true, C is false; thus C did it). B and D contradict each other; therefore, one must be true and one false. Since we've found one true statement (it doesn't matter whether it's B or D), we can deduce that C did it.

Just as some individuals have a math or drawing block, others have a real block against logic problems. They resist a problem like "Who did it?" and often make it more difficult for themselves because they begin with the conviction that it will be hard to do. Be aware of whether you felt a block with any of the exercises. Did you react to any of them by telling yourself you wouldn't do well? If so, you probably didn't, since such negative prophecies usually confirm themselves.

This problem often poses difficulties for people who do not take time to carefully define what they must find for the solution. Some individuals become involved in trying to figure out which statement is true and forget that their goal is to decide which person is guilty. They confuse an information statement with a problem statement. Many students have the same difficulty in solving word problems in school.

If you use this problem with students, you'll find that some of them do an interesting thing with it. They personalize it. They identify the statements with people they know and make arguments such as, "I figured D did it because he sounded suspicious." Understanding a problem in terms of your own experience can be very useful with certain types of problems, but it is a poor way to approach this problem. It's important to help students understand and identify which types of problems a strategy can help with and which ones it cannot. It's also important to help them realize that while "playing a hunch" may be a useful first step in solving a problem, it is always necessary to check that hunch systematically to test its validity.

The problems in the previous exercises are puzzles; they may seem very different from the types of problems you and your students encounter in school and in everyday life. However, the processes you chose to use in solving those puzzles are the same ones you use every day. It is considerably easier to examine those processes in the context of simple puzzles than while dealing with the complexities of real problems. The purpose of the problem-solving exercises is twofold. First, they give you an opportunity to become aware of how you think as well as what you think (process awareness). Second, they are designed to give you some insight into your own individual problem-solving style.

STRATEGIES AND MODES OF THINKING

In working on the preceding exercises, you've had an opportunity to experience your choice of strategies for solving problems. You've also observed the modes of thinking you use most readily. *Modes of thinking* are the languages one uses for thinking—visual imagery, verbal language, mathematics, and kinesthetic and other sensory imagery. *Strategies* are specific techniques for solving problems. There are many different strategies; working forward to reach a solution or backward from an assumed solution are strategies. Which strategy is most efficient depends on the nature of the problem. For example, you've probably seen the kind of problem which shows three fishermen with their lines tangled and asks you to find which fisherman has the fish on the end of his line. If you start following the line from the fisherman, you may have to follow two or three lines to get the solution; however, if you start with the fish you need only trace one line. Mazes are usually solved most easily if one works both forward and backward.

Visualizing, drawing, and charting are all visual strategies. Manipulating objects is a strategy that uses both visual and kinesthetic modes. A strategy like working backward is applicable in all the modes; for example, following the fish back up the line to the fisherman may be done visually or kinesthetically (tracing the line), a math problem like $12 - x = 6$ requires working backward from the solution, and a verbal problem like "Who Did It?" may be solved by assuming that C did it and working backward to check the solution.[5] Being aware of modes of thinking is helpful in understanding learning styles, while an awareness of strategies is useful in analyzing the tasks one asks students to do. To be most effective a teacher must be aware of the strengths and weaknesses of various students as well as of the demands of the tasks being assigned.

Learning Styles.   Modes of thinking are also modes of learning. Most of us rely more heavily on one mode to make meaning of our experience. Many experts classify learners as visual, auditory, or kinesthetic. Although this is clearly an oversimplification, it has real practical utility. To say that a person is primarily visual does not mean that she cannot function effectively in the other modes; it simply indicates her most frequent preference. As you may have discovered in working the problems in the preceding exercises, individuals who have the flexibility to move easily from one mode to another to fit the requirements of the problem will be far more effective at thinking and learning than those who are less flexible and limit themselves to a single mode. The problems should have given you some sense of which modes come most easily to you and which are more difficult.

Understanding the differences in how people think and being aware of one's own personal style and of its strengths and weaknesses is particularly important for teachers. Without that awareness, it is all too easy to assume that the way one approaches a task or problem is the "right" way and to discourage and even penalize other approaches. The result for students whose learning styles differ from the teacher's is to deprive them of their primary and most efficient way of learning. Many cannot overcome this obstacle.

The three diagrams in Figure 3.2 represent a few of the many possible individual learning styles. The individual represented as A is competent in all modes, B is poor in auditory and kinesthetic but competent in visual, C is competent in kinesthetic and visual but outstanding in auditory. A will function well in any classroom, B will only succeed when material is presented visually, and C will be able to learn in any classroom but will do so more quickly and easily when allowed to function in the auditory mode. Being aware of the nature of B's weakness and C's

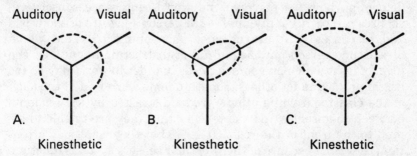

Figure 3.2   In these diagrams each line represents one learning modality. The dotted circle indicates how much the learner uses each modality. If the circle crosses the modality line close to the point where the three lines join, the learner uses that modality so little that it must be considered underdeveloped or impaired. If the dotted circle crosses at the center of the line, the modality is functional; and if it crosses near the far end of the line, it is preferred.

strength will obviously enable the teacher to help each student function more effectively.

Let's look at how an awareness of learning styles and strategies can interact. Spelling can be taught visually (making a visual image), with auditory input (sounding out the word or spelling it aloud in a rhythmic pattern), or kinesthetically (writing or tracing the word a number of times). There is some evidence that the best strategy for spelling is visual; good spellers "see" a mental image of the word.[6] Therefore, teachers should explicitly teach students the strategy of visualizing spelling words—that is, seeing the image of the word in the mind's eye and copying it from there. However, an understanding of learning styles also tells us that some students may have difficulty with a visual strategy and should be encouraged to use an auditory or kinesthetic approach as well. They can copy or sound out the word while still practicing the use of visual imagery. Explicitly teaching an effective strategy while also exploring possible alternatives allows students to develop the individual approaches that work best for them.

The Role of the Sensory System in Learning Style.   One other important component of students' learning styles is the way their sensory systems affect performance in the classroom. Our senses

49

determine how we perceive the world, and since sensory responses are highly individual, each person's picture of the world and responses to it are unique. The volume of sound which pleases one person may be painful or distracting to another; the level of light which one person needs in order to work may be too bright or too dim for others. Some students work well at the back of the classroom while others are so distracted by the students between themselves and the teacher that they are unable to attend to the front of the room. It isn't that they won't pay attention; they *can't* because of the way their sensory systems function.

One child may find it easy to sit still and attend to visual stimuli for forty minutes while a more active seatmate may use so much energy sitting still that there is none left for the learning task. Thirty children may sit in the same classroom, but their experience of that classroom is never exactly the same. It is a different place for the child for whom noise is a compelling and disturbing distraction than for one who has no difficulty screening out irrelevant stimuli. To treat every child exactly the same way is to favor some and penalize others.

A teacher may not be able to meet the needs of all students at all times, but adjustments can be made for individual differences. A classroom can have areas that are quiet in an auditory sense (a no-talking table for those who choose it) and in a visual sense (an area free from visual distractions); seating can be arranged to fit individual needs. Most important of all, the teacher can help students become aware of their individual styles so that they can select the best learning environment and can articulate their needs clearly to other teachers.

TEACHING STUDENTS
PROCESS AWARENESS

While it is essential that teachers be aware of learning styles, it is also important for students to understand their own learning styles and to become aware of modes and strategies they avoid or seldom use. Strategies are the tools of thinking and learning; the more tools we are able to use skillfully, the more successful we will be at a variety of tasks. Despite their importance, strategies are seldom discussed explicitly in class. Even when teachers present a method for solving a specific problem, they seldom take the time to point out other applications of the strategy involved or to ask students if anyone has discovered another strategy or set of strategies that will yield a solution. Without the awareness of how one is approaching a task or problem it's very hard to evaluate and improve performance. Knowing that an answer is right or wrong is often less useful than knowing if a strategy is effective or ineffective. If teachers are to help students develop effective thinking skills, they must not only develop process awareness in themselves but in their students as well. The processes of thinking and learning must be made an explicit part of classroom activities.

Any learning activity provides the potential for process awareness. You can take a few minutes out from a lesson for a discussion of the strategies students are using. For example, in the middle of a science lab or a writing or art project, you can ask students to come together for five to ten minutes to share how they're approaching the problem and air any difficulties they're having. The discussion can occur in the middle of an activity, or it can be sandwiched between two similar activities. Its purpose is to give students an opportunity to explore strategies when they're most immediate and relevant and then to go back to work with new insights and test or apply their learning.[7]

As students become aware of the strategies they use and those they avoid, you can help them begin to assess their own learning styles. If you create a safe environment in which they are not judged or criticized, their own curiosity will be a powerful motivating force. For a student who has always had trouble remembering spoken instructions but who can follow written directions, it can be an exciting revelation to discover that for a particular task his visual system works better than his auditory one. With that information you can help the student develop strategies that use the stronger system (for example, asking the teacher to write things on the board) and encourage him to practice strengthening the weak one.

When you help students discover their own learning styles,

you give them access to tools that they can use in every subject in school and in many situations beyond school. Visual learners may not always be lucky enough to have teachers who are sensitive to their needs, but if they know how to ask for information to be presented in a way that they can learn it, they can educate their teachers to meet their needs. If you've taught them to draw or diagram concepts to help comprehension and memory, they can use that information in other classes as well. They will have learned not only the subject you were teaching but the tools for learning other subjects.

As students develop process awareness, they begin to see the skills you are teaching in a broader context. With this perspective on learning, study is no longer something done to pass a class but an opportunity to gain skills that will make one's life easier and more successful.

SOLUTIONS TO EXERCISES

Exercise 1. The man will take four steps (see Figure 3.3).

Exercise 2. Eight blocks would be painted on three sides, twelve would be painted on two sides, six on one side, and one would be unpainted.

Exercise 3. The paper would be 2^{50} times the original thickness (2^{50} happens to be about 1,100,000,000,000,000). If the original paper was the thickness of typing paper, the answer would be 50,000,000 miles or over half the distance from the earth to the sun. If you have the mathematical facility to solve the problem, it is easy; if not, it is impossible.

Figure 3.3

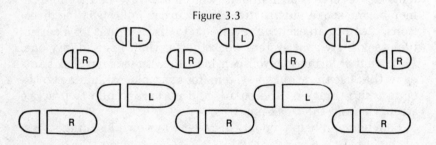

Figure 3.4

Exercise 4. Figure 3.4 shows the solution to the problem.
Exercise 5. C did it.

NOTES

1. Adapted from R. H. McKim, *Experiences in Visual Thinking* (Brooks/Cole, 1972), p. 3, reprinted by permission of the publisher. Copyright © 1972, by Wadsworth Publishing Company.
2. Ibid., p. 9.
3. James L. Adams, *Conceptual Blockbusting: A Guide to Better Ideas,* 2nd ed. (New York: W. W. Norton & Co., Inc., 1979).
4. Lucy Sells, "Math—A Critical Filter," *The Science Teacher,* 45, no. 2 (February 1978).
5. For more information on thinking strategies, see *Strategy Notebook* (San Francisco, Calif.: Interaction Assoc., Inc., 1972) and McKim, *Experiences in Visual Thinking,* pp. 161–65.
6. *Neuro-Linguistic Programming in Education* (Santa Cruz, Calif.: Not Ltd Division of Training and Research, 1980), pp. 13–14.
7. The strategic approach to teaching and the experience-discuss-experience technique which is a part of it were developed by David Straus of Interaction Associates, Inc., as part of *Tools for Change,* a project funded by the Carnegie Corporation.

METAPHOR

What is infinity?

"It's like the Cream of Wheat box, the one with the picture of a boy eating cereal and there's a box of cereal on the table, and the box of cereal has a picture of a box of cereal and that box has a picture . . ."

"It's like amoebas—each amoeba splits and makes two more amoebas and they split and . . ."

"It's like holding a mirror and looking in the mirror—you see the mirror in the mirror in the mirror . . ."

The dictionary defines *infinity* as "the quality of extending beyond measure or comprehension, endless, immeasurable," a verbal, analytical statement which would no doubt please the left hemisphere. The examples given here also describe and explain infinity, but they rely on metaphor, a "language" of both hemispheres. They place the concept within the realm of the concrete world, forging a connection between the abstract concept and the learner's experience. They are, for most people, more engaging and satisfying than the exacting, one-dimensional dictionary definition. They both clarify the concept and tease the mind to explore it further.

Imagine for a moment the difference between a class where students are introduced to the concept of the infinity of space through the dictionary definition and a few textbook examples, such as the size of the universe and the duration of time, and a class in which the teacher brings in two mirrors and initiates discussion of the metaphors given here as a means of exploring the concept of limitlessness and immeasurability, then asks the students to generate more metaphors of their own. The latter would not only be more interesting but is also likely to produce a deeper and clearer understanding of infinity. It presents students with the concept in ways that make sense in terms of their own experience and challenges them to use the process of metaphorical thinking to extend their understanding. It also enables the teacher to assess exactly how well they understand the concept from the metaphors they offer and to clarify confusion by referring to the student-generated metaphors.

What exactly is metaphorical thinking? It is the ability to make connections between two unlike things by recognizing that in some way they share a common trait or exemplify a common principle. For example, the fuel filter of an internal combustion engine is like the kidneys of a human in that they both serve the function of filtering wastes, and they accomplish this filtration by sorting molecules. Certain molecules pass through; others are retained. The kidneys might also be compared to a coffee filter, to a gravel screen or egg sorter, or to the system of parking stickers which admits certain cars to a parking lot. None of these things is *exactly* like a kidney, but a discussion of the ways each one is similar and different would elicit a good deal of information about kidneys and how they function. To give some examples from other subjects, a revolution can be compared to a volcano (pressures building toward explosion), narrative writing to a chain with the transitions being the links, theme and variation to the Thanksgiving turkey and the endless ways of preparing its leftovers, and electricity to water running through pipes.

In Chapter 1, it was suggested that the right hemisphere may function like a kaleidoscope. The purpose of offering that metaphor was to provide a single image which would draw together the attributes of the right hemisphere (simultaneous, nonlinear processing, and constant combining and recombining of many parts to create a vast variety of visual, spatial patterns or wholes). Right-hemisphere processing is not exactly like a kaleidoscope (indeed, we do not yet know how it functions), but the metaphor serves several useful purposes. It provides an extremely efficient way to organize and remember information. In place of a list of separate attributes, it offers a single image which contains most of the attributes. Like the containerized boxcars that can move from ship to train or truck, it enables you to deal with a single whole instead of its many constituent parts. The metaphor also creates a link between the list of attributes and your own experience. If you've seen a kaleidoscope and know how it works, you can use that knowledge to help you understand the new, unfamiliar concept of right-hemisphere processing. Your own experience is brought into the learning process, and the connections between that experience and the new concept make learning easier and more efficient.

Take a moment to experience metaphorical thinking for yourself. You have been reading about the hemispheres of the brain and two modes of thinking; you are at a point in your own learning process not unlike the one your students experience toward the end of a unit. As you answer the following questions, remember that there are no right answers.

EXERCISE 1

1. What animal is like the right hemisphere? Why? How is it different? What animal is like the left hemisphere? Why? How is it different?
2. If your school were a person, what would be its right hemisphere? What would be its left hemisphere? Why?
3. The relationship between the right and left hemisphere is like the one between _____ and _____ because _____

The purpose of these questions is not to test your knowledge (though your answers would provide some indication of that); it is to give you new ways to think about what you already know and to enable you to experience metaphorical thinking applied to a learning situation. It's unfortunate that you can't discuss your answers with others doing the same exercise since discovering and responding to connections quite different from one's own contributes substantially to the learning process. At the end of this chapter you'll find responses from several other teachers, but please don't read them until you've done the exercise yourself.

ADVANTAGES OF METAPHORICAL TEACHING

Teaching through metaphor is not a new process; good teachers have always helped students grasp new ideas by explaining them in terms of something the students already understood. Yet even very skillful teachers seldom teach metaphorical thinking explicitly so that their students can make this valuable tool a part of their own repertoire of mental skills. To offer students a connection is only the beginning of teaching through metaphor; it provides a model of metaphorical thinking, but it does not teach the skill. To do that one must ask students to generate and discuss metaphors themselves. There are many ways to do this. The most direct way is to ask what students know that is like the thing being studied, how it is similar and how different from that thing.[1] One should not be deceived by the simplicity with which the process can be described; to listen for students' connections and help them articulate and clarify their thoughts requires skill and practice and produces very basic changes in a classroom.

Metaphor is probably the most powerful of the right-hemisphere techniques because it makes explicit the process by which learning occurs. In a traditional classroom students are left to make their own connections. Those who do not make the connections flounder. They are playing a game in which no one has thought to tell them the rules. In introducing metaphorical thinking into the instructional process, the teacher gives them training in using the strategies which their more successful classmates have intuitively discovered. Those already skilled at making connections as part of their own learning process also benefit because metaphorical teaching reinforces the process and makes it more accessible to conscious use.

Metaphorical teaching is also more efficient because it recognizes that new information need not be taught from "scratch" and makes use of what students *already* know. Linear, textbook presentations separate and compartmentalize knowledge, confronting students with a great mass of information which can often be overwhelming. In contrast, metaphors organize and connect information. Once students understand that the development of a seed to a flowering plant is somewhat like that of an egg into a chicken, what they know about the development of eggs can be used to help them learn about seeds. In addition, studying the new subject (seeds) in terms of the known (eggs) reinforces previous learning. Figure 4.1 represents visually the difference between the two approaches.

The metaphorical mode of teaching is holistic; it constantly focuses on the processes of recognizing and understanding patterns and general principles which give meaning to specific facts. Each new unit is no longer an isolated set of information but an opportunity to make new connections, to gain insight into both the new subject and that which is already known. If spiders are

Figure 4.1   In the traditional approach, knowledge is separated into categories and each subject presents itself as something entirely new to be learned. Metaphorical teaching emphasizes connections—how the subject is like something already understood. The area where the circles overlap represents how seeds and eggs are alike, e.g., they have many of the same needs, similar parts, similar patterns of development. In these areas, students' understanding of eggs can be applied to the new material they must learn.

Traditional Approach

Metaphorical Approach

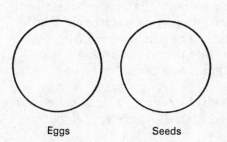
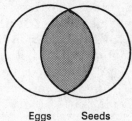

Eggs   Seeds   Eggs   Seeds

only important during the unit on arachnids, the information about them can be memorized and forgotten; however, if students hear them referred to by classmates in terms of other units and even other subjects, it becomes both more important and easier to learn and remember information about them. Learning has a sense of integration when the emphasis is on seeing relationships; it is both more efficient and more satisfying.

When students are encouraged to propose their own metaphors, they are invited to bring their own experience into the classroom. This is a dramatic departure from traditional approaches where school is kept separate from the rest of a student's life. Traditional techniques usually ignore the students' experience and present information to them as though they were blank books and knowledge was imparted only in the classroom. In reality, even kindergartners come to school with a rich fund of experience and a repertoire of strategies for understanding the world. When their experience and strategies are devalued by being ignored, students learn that life and school are separate and that all their learning outside school is useless in the classroom (and often vice versa). Science becomes what is done in science period, but not what happens as they muck about the garden or vacant lot watching bugs and spiders. It is not only inefficient to ignore knowledge which students already possess; it also creates a conflict between two areas that should be reinforcing each other rather than competing and makes it easier for less successful students to withdraw from and reject school learning. Bright, competent, streetwise kids become academic underachievers.

Finally, using metaphor makes learning easier because it provides a context for asking questions. If a student doesn't understand a textbook or lecture, he frequently has trouble identifying his problem clearly enough to ask for help, and "I don't understand" doesn't help the teacher identify the source of confusion. Metaphors, by their nature, suggest questions. "Is it like X in this way?" "X does such-and-such, does Y?" A high school teacher who began to use metaphor reported that within a month or two students started coming to him with questions like, "I understand that up to this point, it's like _____, right? What I don't understand is _____." He estimated that at least 70 percent of his students were using metaphorical thinking on their own. Students who understand the material being taught find that metaphors suggest such questions as "If X is like Y in this way, is it like Y in this other way?" or "So X and Y are sorters. What are the exact mechanisms they use to sort? Are they the same?" Their questions take them beyond the book to discover more than the information given. Thus, the same technique is helpful to both low and high achievers.

USING METAPHOR
IN THE CLASSROOM

Metaphors can be used effectively at all stages of instruction. Later in this chapter we'll explore exactly how to apply them to introducing, clarifying, reviewing, and testing material as well as stimulating writing. Before studying applications, however, let's examine how to generate and select a metaphor and how to encourage students to produce their own metaphors.

Generating Metaphors. A good metaphor can be immensely helpful when new material is introduced to students. How does one find a good metaphor—that is, one which is familiar to the class and contains sufficient parallels to the subject? If you're fairly intuitive, it may just "come" to you. In that case it's still important not to skip over the process of analyzing your metaphor; it may be excellent for your purposes, but you are unlikely to get its full value if you are unclear on exactly what you're using it to teach. If you're not particularly intuitive, you can still generate metaphors, and you'll find that the process gets easier the more you do it. In fact, while you may have to work to find metaphors at first, after some practice they'll begin to come to you quickly and even spontaneously.

Let's go back to the example of the lesson on kidneys presented earlier to see how one might go about selecting and analyzing a metaphor. Here's an example of a dialogue you might have with yourself.

1. What do I want students to know about the kidneys?
   How they function and their importance to the body.
2. How do they function?
   They filter wastes.
3. How do they filter wastes?
   They sort molecules: Some pass through, some are retained. (*In an advanced class you might want to be even more specific about this point.*)
4. What's their importance to the body?
   They remove wastes so the blood can carry more nutrients and pick up more wastes.
5. What can I think of that filters wastes by sorting out something (in other words, that functions like a kidney)?(*At this point just sit and let ideas come to you. Don't force them; be receptive to images or vaguely formed ideas.*)
   A fuel filter, or a coffee filter for that matter.
   Different kinds of sorters—a gravel screen, an egg sorter, an IBM card sorter that selects any card that has a certain pattern of holes punched on it.
   A parking lot where cars with certain stickers are admitted.
   School games where you need a student body card to get in.
6. All my metaphors are sorters. Do any of them purify a circulating system?
   The fuel filter does.
7. Is everyone in the class familiar enough with a fuel filter to understand the metaphor?
   No.
8. Okay, we can still use it to clarify things later, but let's find a clear metaphor to introduce the idea.
   How about a gravel sorter? I can demonstrate that so that they can *see* how the sorting works. If I can't get that, I can use a coffee filter, though I'll have to make it clear that the kidneys don't sort on the basis of solids versus liquids.
9. How is the gravel sorter different from the kidneys?
   It's not part of a circulating system.
   Its sorting is much simpler than the kidneys; the gravel sorter uses the sole criterion of size, while the kidney uses much more complex criteria.
10. How do I put this all together?

First, I'll use the gravel sorter or coffee filter to introduce the concept of sorting and separating and will explore how the metaphor fits and how it doesn't (degree of complexity in criteria for sorting, not part of circulating system).

I'll talk about other sorters and ask students for examples. We'll compare their sorters to kidneys.

I'll ask for examples of sorters that purify a circulating system. If they have trouble, I can ask for examples of circulating systems and then ask them to find the thing in the system that filters wastes. If necessary, I can suggest the fuel filter or the swimming pool filter.

The dialogue illustrates one way you might go about selecting a metaphor and planning a lesson around it. The process can be simplified into three steps:

1. Decide exactly what you want to teach and what general principle is involved (questions 1–4).
2. Generate metaphors, select the one which best communicates the concept you've chosen to teach, and clarify the discrepancies, that is, the ways in which the metaphor does not fit the subject (questions 5–9).
3. Make a lesson plan which includes how you'll elicit metaphors from students (question 10, especially part 3).

It's terribly tempting to think up a metaphor in the five minutes before class and go with it. Teachers who are experienced in metaphor can get away with that. However, lacking experience, most of us ordinary mortals get caught; we suddenly discover that the metaphor doesn't fit quite as well as we'd thought or that the point it teaches is not the one we wanted to focus on, or the students start suggesting metaphors, and we don't quite know what to do with them. Those are all problems which can result when you're not really clear on what it is you're teaching, and once you're confused, your students are confused.

Setting Content Goals. In knowing exactly what to teach and keeping a clear focus, science teachers are at an advantage. The subject matter of science is much more clearly defined than that of history or social studies. There is an accepted concept of what students should know about the kidneys and how they function; in history there is no such consensus about the Civil War, for example. Historians do not agree on what is most important to know about this period of history, or whether the causes were primarily economic, social, or political, or on the motivations of various groups and individuals. The dates, places, and outcomes of battles are known, but teachers differ on their view of the importance of knowing about these battles. It is much easier to answer, "What do I want students to know about the kidneys?" than "What do I want them to know about the Civil War?"

Textbooks are seldom any help; they offer a linear presentation of facts and concepts with little help in how one selects what is important to give the subject meaning. This is why history is so often taught as a chronology of dates and facts to memorize; it takes a gifted and dedicated teacher to organize all that information so that it takes on meaning. But it can be done, and one place to start is by forcing yourself to constantly clarify what you want students to understand. "To learn about the Panama Canal" is not a teaching objective. What do you want students to know about the Canal? "The role of the Canal in world commerce and in the growth of the United States as a world power" is still not an objective because it is too general. What was the Canal's role? Exactly what part did it play in world events? If you find yourself resisting answering questions like "What role did the Canal play?" you should consider the possibility that you may not be absolutely clear on the role and you need to specify the answer for yourself. Some teachers resist being specific in content goals because they don't want to leave anything out. They feel that by keeping their goals general, they allow themselves and their students more freedom to explore all aspects of the subject. Specific objectives do not limit freedom. In fact, they provide a structure within which one may explore the subject without becoming confused and losing sight of the main points. Students can challenge a clear objective and test their powers of critical thinking. If the teacher fails to decide what is important to know, students become easily confused. After all, if the teacher cannot articulate what it is that one should know about the Panama Canal, how can students be expected to answer that question? The more specific your teaching goals, the clearer your teaching will be and the easier it will be to generate and use metaphors.

It's important to realize that selecting content goals is one of a teacher's most difficult jobs. In a traditional, linear approach a teacher can often get away with setting goals from the text ("Students will know the information on pages 117 to 133") and testing on the content of a book. But at best such an approach teaches memorization and is unlikely to produce in-depth understanding of the subject. Therefore, whether you use metaphor or not, the process of clarifying your goals is an important one.

One very useful technique which can be used in any subject to help you define what you want to teach is to ask how the thing is different from everything else like it.[2] If you know what made World War II different from other wars, you've identified qualities which it is important for students to understand. In psychology you can ask how Jungian theory is different from the other major psychological theories, and the answer will provide a definition of Jungian theory. It will also help students understand the relationship between the schools of thought or the historical phenomena they're studying. It both clarifies and integrates.

Common Problems. There are several problems you may encounter when you begin using metaphor; most are a result of content goals that are not absolutely clear.

1. You can't find a metaphor that fits what you want to teach.

   You may be trying to teach too many things at once. Ask yourself what's the most important thing for students to understand and look for a metaphor for that; other points may be worked in as discrepancies.

2. Questions arise about the analogue that confuse you or the class.

   Either you or your students may not know enough about the analogue you've chosen. If students know more about the analogue than you, ask them to help clarify, but keep focusing on the general principle you want to teach. If students are unfamiliar with your analogue, use another one or back off from metaphor until you can find one they're familiar with.

3. Students become so interested in the analogue that they generate too many ideas and discussion wanders and loses focus.

Metaphors are seductive; they can lead in many directions. You can help clarify connections by noting them on the blackboard. Be sure to sum up by stressing the main points you want remembered and other *significant* points that may have been suggested.

4. Students generate metaphors based on connections that are not of primary importance.

This is not a problem as long as *you* clarify for the class the relative importance of connections for understanding the subject. Be sure to reward even less effective metaphors; they demonstrate metaphorical thinking and should be encouraged. *Never put down or ignore a student's metaphor.*

The degree to which the use of analogy is effective depends to a great extent on the students' experience. If you're using the metaphor of an engine with a student whose passion is fixing cars, the response is apt to be very positive not only because you've chosen something the student is interested in but because he has a rich body of experience with which to think about the new subject and is apt to come up with questions and generate insights a less mechanically minded student would miss.

Helping Students Generate Metaphors.   The problem of finding the "right" metaphor for each student is easily solved when you allow students to suggest their own metaphors based on their experience. In asking for metaphors, you not only insure that the students have had direct experience with the analogue and are interested in it, but you also give them direct, explicit training in metaphorical thinking. In fact, while selecting good metaphors to present material is important, getting students to offer their own metaphors makes a far more significant contribution to the learning process.

An analogy is never exactly like the thing to which it's being compared; there are always discrepancies. In developing metaphors to teach something, the teacher needs to look for the closest "fit" possible—that is, the analogue that is most like the subject. The closer the analogy, the less possibility for confusion. However, student-generated analogies do not need to have the same close "fit" as teaching analogies. Students can demonstrate an excellent grasp of the subject even with a relatively poor analogue if they can articulate clearly how their analogue is like and unlike the subject. The analogue itself is not nearly as important as the thinking behind it. For this reason it is essential to ask for similarities and discrepancies when a student offers an analogy. Once the class has had some experience in metaphor, you'll find students beginning to "piggyback" on each other's answers by suggesting other similarities and discrepancies missed by the originator. The mind play involved in such interchanges not only is enjoyable but contributes to everyone's understanding of the subject.

Some students may propose excellent metaphors but fall silent when you ask how the subject is like and unlike the analogue. For some, the problem is one of self-confidence; they may feel they're being asked to defend their answer and are fearful of making a mistake. For others, the problem is more complicated. They may have derived the metaphor intuitively and are unable to verbalize the reasons for their choice. In such cases you can help them by supporting the validity of their response while asking questions to help them translate their ideas into words. If "How is X like Y?" draws a blank, try "What does X do that's like what Y does?" or "What does X do? Does Y do anything like that?" It's also important to help students elaborate on their metaphors. Encourage them to find more than one important similarity and to explore fully the discrepancies. The more mileage they can get from a metaphor, the sharper their thinking is becoming.

The importance of listening carefully and sensitively to student responses cannot be overemphasized. In most teaching techniques the emphasis is on the teacher's presentation of information; teaching with metaphor places an equal or even greater emphasis on listening skills. You are no longer listening for an answer but for the thinking behind the answer. You cannot assume that a student suggesting a metaphor is making the same connection you are, so you must ask for the connection. Helping students articulate their connections may seem a bit tedious at times, but it is still an efficient use of teaching time since it helps develop important thinking skills and also reinforces the substantive learning for the rest of the class. In addition, it may lead to the discovery that some students who seem hopelessly dull are much brighter than they've appeared.

An example of the importance of listening and probing with questions occurred in a first-grade Title I class that used metaphorical thinking as part of a project designed by Synectics Education Systems (SES).[3] The teacher had asked which of several things in the American Indians' environment might have given them the idea for one of their inventions. One boy suggested that the turtle's shell might have led to the tepee. The look on the teacher's face revealed that this was not the answer she'd expected (the shield looked more like the shell and was the more obvious answer). However, she'd been trained to listen and ask questions, so she asked how it might have led to the tepee. The boy responded that the shell protected the turtle from the rain and snow, and the tepee protected the Indians the same way. The teacher's surprise and delight at his response were probably the most positive reinforcement that the boy had gotten in his entire school career. That experience of being listened to encouraged him to risk expressing his ideas more frequently, and the teacher's discovery of the folly of judging too quickly helped her listen more carefully not only to him but to the other students as well.

Introducing Material.   In introducing material teachers face two kinds of problems—either students are completely unfamiliar with the subject and need help in relating it to something they already understand, or they're so familiar with it that it does not engage their interest. The problems may seem diametrically opposed, but metaphor can be helpful in solving both of them. We've already discussed how it can be used in the first instance. Now let's look at how it can be used to generate involvement.

A high school science teacher wanted students to become really involved in the dissection of a clam, and he knew that at best the assignment usually evoked a going-through-the-motions response. So he introduced the unit with a discussion of fear—no mention of clams, just an exploration of situations in which students had experienced fear and how their bodies had reacted to it: curling up, protecting the face, and so on. With the students fully involved in their discussion of fear, he moved on to ask, "What animals are shaped by fear?" and next, "What human inventions have been shaped by fear?" Finally he put those questions together and asked, "Which animal corresponds to which invention?" The answer to his question provided an inventory of the forms that fear can take. The next day he confronted the class with the clams and asked them to identify ten fear-formed structures. The clams were no longer an assignment to be gotten through but a genuine intellectual challenge, an opportunity for students to test their observations against their own ideas. As one might expect, the assignment was done with a good deal of careful attention and enthusiasm.[4]

Jack Stovel of Mt. Greylock High School in Williamstown, Massachusetts, launched his world history classes on an investigation of the French Revolution by exploring the power structure of the school. Once the students became interested in exploring how power operated in their own institution, they were far more interested in the power struggles of eighteenth-century France. Instead of memorizing the Three Estates and the roles each played, students looked for analogues in the school, explored the power relations between groups, and related them to the situation in France. By the end of the unit they not only had learned some history and a bit of sociology, but also had developed an understanding of power and how it functions that was useful in future history units.

These two lessons work so well because their originators were very clear on what they wanted to teach and took the time to make connections which focused on an area of their students' experience which was meaningful in terms of that concept. The inspiration for the science teacher's lesson came when he looked at the clam and observed what a fearful fellow it is. He was well aware that fear was something teenagers could relate to. The history teacher had decided that one of the things students should get from history is an understanding of power and how it operates. He was clear on what he thought could be learned about power by studying the French Revolution, so he was able to find metaphors appropriate to his subject.

Structuring, Clarifying, and Reviewing.   Metaphor serves many purposes—from a quick example to clarify a specific point to a device for structuring an entire unit. When you use metaphor to structure a unit, you integrate information in an extremely efficient manner which makes it much easier for students to remember. If they've forgotten a specific point, they can use the metaphor to rediscover it. Gene Davis of Albany High School in Albany, California, presents the circulatory system by using the metaphor of a road system. The arteries are freeways, arterials are off-ramps, and capillaries are city streets. Vehicles (blood cells) must be on city streets (capillaries) to do their work; they deliver some things and pick up others. As he introduces the organs associated with the circulatory system and their functions, he helps students to fit them into the metaphor. Like any good metaphor, the system of roads offers rich possibilities for creative teaching.

Whether you use metaphor to introduce a unit, clarify a concept, or review, the process is the same. The difference is the point at which the metaphor is brought into the lesson. Metaphors for introducing material are usually teacher generated; those for review are more often student generated. Near the end of a unit it can be very useful to give a written assignment asking students to suggest a metaphor for the subject you're studying ("What do you know that's like _____?" "How is it like _____?" "How is it different?"). You can select a student metaphor from the papers and use it to review with the class. The assignment should help you assess the class's understanding of the subject and clarify points that may be causing confusion. Such papers are also a good way to enable students to practice metaphorical and writing skills in preparation for possible future tests. (See "Evaluating Metaphors" in this chapter for suggestions on how to evaluate and use such assignments to sharpen metaphorical skills.)

Testing. Most tests are a major waste of teaching time. While the need to study may produce some learning, the actual taking of the test is "dead time" in terms of learning. When material is tested in the same form in which it was presented, students are encouraged to memorize and repeat what they've learned. That process does not require any new thinking; often, it doesn't even require that students understand the material. However, questions which require students to apply their knowledge to a new problem or to translate it into a different form force them beyond memorization and provide a much more accurate evaluation of their comprehension. They are also more challenging to the student and transform the testing situation into an opportunity to practice valuable skills.

Questions based on metaphors are an excellent way to evaluate comprehension. Compare, for example, the following two questions from a history exam:

1. List the major events leading up to the French Revolution and explain their importance.
2. How was the period leading up the French Revolution like the building up of a thunderstorm? Be sure to include in your analogy the major events leading up to the Revolution.

A student might memorize the answer to the first question, but not the second. The analogy question requires that students not only know the events leading up to the Revolution but understand them well enough to explain their significance in terms of something else, in this case a thunderstorm. You can suggest the metaphor and ask for connections, or you can allow students to generate their own metaphors and connections, but the latter is more difficult and should not be done until students have had a good deal of experience with metaphor.

One word of caution is in order when you begin to use new techniques like metaphor as evaluative tools. Many students are likely to be extremely threatened if the new techniques are thrust upon them too quickly. They may feel you're changing the rules of the game, and they will resent the change. In addition, many students have worked hard to master traditional tests, and they may feel that the new technique places them at a disadvantage. It is best for everyone if you give students a chance to practice answering metaphorical questions a number of times before using them on a test. You can also begin by giving students a choice between a question phrased traditionally and one based on metaphor. As students become experienced in answering these types of questions, they can become a regular part of your tests.

Stimulating Writing. When you use metaphor to teach, you are also providing students with a powerful model for their own writing since the process of expository writing, that is, presenting information clearly and in a form that promotes understanding, frequently relies on metaphor. You can make this process explicit by giving writing assignments which require students to use metaphor to explain something. Have them select a concept or fact to explain to someone (the someone should be a specific person or group of people). Ask them to write a sentence or two telling exactly what they want to communicate, to select an analogue that their audience will understand, and to write a paragraph using the analogue to explain their fact or concept.[5]

In creative writing, metaphor serves a very different purpose than it does in learning and in expository writing. In the latter two, the purpose is to clarify by helping the listener make connections with something which is familiar. SES calls this "making the strange familiar." In creative writing the goal is to see things in a new way and to make a connection that is original and enlightening—what SES calls "making the familiar strange." To achieve this one must break preconceived connections and generate new and unusual ones. Metaphor can provide a structure for making new connections. When you ask students what animal is like anger and how (not what animal is angry but which is *like* anger in some way), you get past their usual pattern of response and suggest a way for them to explore the subject that may produce fresh insight.

The following paragraphs by a sixth-grade student illustrate the impact of metaphorical training on creativity in writing. The first was written before exposure to metaphorical materials, the second after a series of lessons using metaphor.

> Zero is a number that is nothing. It is used as a place holder. It is round, like a tire or a lifesaver. Even though Zero is nothing, you've got to have it for arithmetic. It looks exactly like the letter O. When Zero is used to multiply, the answer is always Zero. When Zero comes after a number, it makes that number ten times bigger.
>
> Zero is like a water well because both are pretty important holes. Zero is helpful when it jumps behind another number and makes it bigger. It is a killer when you multiply by it. If I were Zero, I would roll away whenever they tried to make me multiply. Or I would grow a tail to look like a nine. I don't even want to be a helpful killer such as Zero.[6]

The second paragraph demonstrates clear growth in the student's ability to use metaphor and a resultant improvement in the quality of his writing.

One of the first steps in using metaphorical materials is to help students loosen up. You must prove to them several times that they needn't worry about making mistakes, that there is no "correct" answer for your questions. If you ask a question like "What color is sleep?" or "Which weighs more—a boulder or a heavy heart?" there is no hidden right answer. In fact, the answer is unimportant; the reasons for the answer are far more interesting. The playful quality of such questions helps students relax their tight control and encourages their aesthetic selves to take over. SES refers to this type of question as a "stretching exercise," an invitation to stretch the mind and discover one's own creativity. The following exercises can be used with any age group; they should give you an idea of how to design questions of your own.[7]

1. If the ocean were a sea of teachers, what do you imagine the foam would be made of?[8]
2. Which is softer—a *whisper* or a *kitten's fur*?

3. Which is more *curious*—a *monkey* or a *root?*
4. How is a *beaver chewing on a log* like a *typewriter?*
5. A clock acts like ＿＿＿＿ because ＿＿＿＿.[9]
6. What animal is like a rubber band?
7. What kind of animal are you most like?[10]

English Classes.   Metaphor plays a special role in English classes since the study of poetry and literature often becomes a study
of metaphor. In studying poetry like Shakespeare's Sonnet XVIII,
students must be able to understand the meaning of the poet's
comparison of his love to a summer's day. In *Moby Dick* the entire
novel takes on a metaphorical form as the quest for the great
white whale comes to represent a great deal more than a whaling
voyage. Even in less obviously metaphorical works, there is often
a metaphorical level. Authors select subjects and develop them in
a particular way in order to address the issues which concern
them. Anne Rice, author of *Interview with a Vampire* and *The
Feast of All Saints,* speaks of looking for "wells of metaphor,"
subjects through which she can explore the themes that have
power for her.[11] One way to deepen students' understanding of
literature and help them engage the themes of a given work is to
make them aware of this metaphorical level.

Many teachers approach metaphors in literature by asking
students to analyze them, leaving some students with the mis-
taken idea that metaphors are generated analytically. Since metaphors are a product of associative thinking, they can also be
understood in this way. You can ask students what the metaphor
suggests to them, what images or sounds or feelings it stimulates.
In doing this, you work from the students' experience and associations. Several students sharing their ideas can discover which of
their responses are idiosyncratic and which are shared by others.
The latter can provide insight into the metaphor's meaning.

One teacher who wanted students to appreciate the strength
of metaphor in poetry introduced her lesson with a short fantasy.
She asked students to imagine themselves in a garden and to see
a beautiful rosebush covered with deep red roses. She had them
smell and touch the roses and examine them from many sides.
Then while their eyes were still closed, she read Robert Burns'

"My Love Is Like a Red, Red Rose." Afterward they discussed how their fantasy experience had affected their response to the poem and used their associations to decide what the poet meant to communicate. They explored how the meaning would be changed if the metaphor for love were a yellow rose or a daisy or a jasmine blossom. From a lesson like this one it is an easy step to having students use metaphor as a base for their own poetry and prose.

Integrating Different Subjects. Elementary school teachers have a particular advantage in using metaphor and other right-hemisphere techniques. Since they teach a variety of subjects, they can organize their teaching to integrate different areas of curriculum. For example, the exercise on zero quoted in the section on "Stimulating Writing" functions as both a math and writing lesson. SES has a unit that integrates math, science, history, music, and writing.[12] Students study about how amoebas divide to reproduce themselves while in American history they're studying the colonial period. They compare the amoeba with the Massachusetts Bay Colony and discuss how the divisions of the amoeba and of the colony were similar and different. They fold paper to understand exponential growth and discuss why the mathematics of amoeba colonies is not quite like that of the folding paper. They do some expository writing and some fanciful writing ("If the American colonies were made of cheese, who would be the mice?" "If amoebas ate light bulbs, what would happen when they reproduced?"). And, finally, they listen to Beethoven's Fifth Symphony, become aware of its variations on a theme, and write about how what they heard in the music is like amoebas reproducing. The SES unit is an ambitious one, and a beginner should not try to work with so many elements. You can make a good start with this type of teaching by looking for two areas that can be integrated. If you're studying local history, such as how your town or state has grown to its present form, you might also do a science unit on the growth of tadpoles to frogs. Those two subjects will provide opportunities for comparisons that will enrich both units and will provide insight into the processes of growth.

In junior and senior high it's more difficult to integrate different subject areas, but it's not impossible. If your school has requirements which place the majority of students in a given subject at a given time—for example, sophomores in biology, juniors in American history—you will at least be able to find out what many of your students are studying in another subject; you may find that knowledge useful in selecting metaphors. When more than one teacher in a school begins using metaphorical techniques, students experience the connection of process across subjects. It's very exciting for them to discover that the same tool they used in science can be used in history.

Early Elementary Grades.   Metaphor has special importance for teachers of young children. For one thing, it's an excellent way to explain new ideas (many parents and primary teachers use it extensively without even being conscious of it); but even more importantly, for some primary students explicit training in metaphorical thinking skills can dramatically improve achievement in school. In a Title I project in Lawrence, Massachusetts, SES introduced connection-making lessons daily to 100 students in kindergarten through third grade. The lessons began with simple connection making such as associating an object with the sound it makes and recognizing similarities and differences between a dog and a cat, a horse and a cow, a wolf and a shark, and so on. Students progressed from simple sensory connections to functional ones—for example, seeing that a wolf and a shark are both predators. The lessons also included training in personal analogy (or identification fantasy) to enable the students to identify with an animate or inanimate object at an emotional and kinesthetic level. The four-month project produced dramatic results. For first graders' increases over the previous year's scores (the same Title I project without connection making) were 286 percent in aural comprehension, 1,038 percent in word reading, and 163 percent in sentence reading.[13]

In trying to understand how this dramatic improvement occurred, the SES team theorized that the children had suffered a breakdown in their metaphorical processes.

> To sum up—our analysis of these culturally deprived students is that their natural, innate connection-making process

was short-circuited. They devaluated their background so savagely that they blocked out their source of connections. They sublimated all aspects of this unbearably painful connection source. Thus, their whole connection-making process was repressed and they were unable to learn.[14]

A further factor in the students' improvement may have been their discovery that their teachers were actually listening to them. A primary cause for many students' seeming inability to express themselves is their perception that teachers don't really listen to them. Too often teachers listen for answers, not for what a student thinks. Once students realize this, they have the choice of either trying to figure out the answer the teacher wants or of playing dumb and refusing to participate. If they choose the latter course of action, or inaction, they have little motivation to listen or express themselves.

Using traditional materials and approaches, it is extremely difficult *not* to listen for answers and discourage responses which diverge from the expected information. Students learn about right answers very early in their schooling. The SES project offered teachers and students a way to break this pattern. By providing materials designed to elicit multiple connections along with training which encouraged teachers to probe students' answers in order to understand each learner's connections, SES made a subtle but essential change in the gestalt of the classroom. Teachers began to listen to students, and once students recognized this change, they began to listen to teachers and to try to express their thoughts.

It has been popular to refer to lower-class and minority children as "culturally deprived." The SES experience makes it clear that though their environment and experiences are different from those of their more affluent classmates and most of their teachers, their background is no less rich in material for metaphor. It is not experience that they lack as much as the encouragement to bring that experience into the classroom and make use of it there. One of the exciting side effects of the SES project was that parents reported that their children discussed their school experience much more at home. Since the children's experience formed the basis for the lessons, their schoolwork became much more comprehensible to their parents, and alienation from the school was reduced.

Evaluating Metaphors. Evaluation is frequently a matter of assessing what students do wrong. The teacher notes that they've failed to learn something and then goes on to the next unit. Processes are not learned at one sitting, and they are important enough to deserve attention over time. In evaluating students' metaphorical abilities (and all other right-hemisphere processes), try to view your job not as judging proficiency so much as assessing what students need to help them improve. If a student has trouble analyzing discrepancies in metaphors, don't consider this to be a statement of ability but rather a sign that the student needs further work in that area. If you adopt this attitude to evaluation, you will give all your students the time and help to develop their abilities at their own pace, and it's very likely that by the end of the year your entire class will be skillful in metaphorical thinking.

Using metaphor in school is a new skill for most students, and it's best to give them plenty of practice before you do an evaluation. Both in classroom discussion and written assignments you'll need to familiarize students with the process and to help them develop confidence in their ability to use it. Trust is a crucial factor in this process. Students must feel safe to respond in new and unfamiliar ways in a classroom; they must know that they will not be ridiculed for mistakes. One way to help students sharpen their skills without being critical is to look for what they do right and build on that. If a child suggests a visual connection when you consider a functional one to be more important, you can reward the student for making the connection and also ask if she can think of a way the two things are similar in what they do. When you're working with metaphor, never put down a student's connection and never ignore it (a failure to respond is a negative response). The process of learning to make connections is far more important than the specific content of a given lesson.

As in any other skill there are levels of sophistication in metaphor. For most children visual connections (a cat and a dog both have four feet) are the first and easiest. Other sensory connections (they both have soft fur, but their tongues feel different, or they both growl but a dog barks and a cat meows) come next. Functional metaphors (a cat and a dog are both pets; they both do useful things for people) are more difficult and generally more useful. We tend to consider the essence of most things to be more closely related to what they do than to how they appear.[15] If you have students who consistently offer sensory connections, you can help them move to functional ones with questions like "Can you think of something that these two things do that's the same?" or "What does X do that's like what Y does?"

When you're using metaphor to teach substantive material, you can evaluate whether or not the students' connections are based on what you consider an important aspect of the subject. The Bill of Rights is like a turkey because they both developed in North America, but that is not a major connection. If you get an answer like that, ask the students what's important about the Bill of Rights (don't expect a good answer unless your teaching was clear on that point), and then ask if they can think of something that's similar in that way. For example, if a student answers that the Bill of Rights limits the power of government and protects the basic rights of citizens, you might ask what animal protects something small by limiting the power of something large. Once you have an answer, you can ask how the animal's means of protection is like the Bill of Rights' protection and how it's different. Asking what's important focuses attention on a major aspect of the subject, and suggesting an analogy to an animal gives the students a structure for their answers.

If you're evaluating a written response to a metaphor question (again, don't do this until you've done a good deal of work with metaphor in class and you know students are able to generate connections and analyze similarities and differences), your focus should be on how well the student uses the metaphor to discuss the important points about the subject being studied. You can make a list of the things that should be included (either as similarities or differences from the analogue) and check each answer against it. Then you can give extra points for a particularly apt or creative metaphor. If there are five points you consider important, it doesn't matter whether a student offers a metaphor which covers four of them as similar and one as discrepant or a metaphor which covers one as similar and four as discrepant.

Both answers demonstrate an equal grasp of the material; the former demonstrates a superior ability in metaphorical thinking. You should decide in advance whether and how much you want to reward metaphorical thinking.

CONCLUSION

Aristotle commented, "The greatest thing by far is to be a master of metaphor. It is the one thing which cannot be learned from others. It is a mark of genius." Fortunately, even great philosophers are sometimes wrong. For while Aristotle's respect for metaphorical thinking was certainly justified, his pessimism about the possibility of teaching and learning that process were not. As this chapter has shown, metaphor can become an integral part of the learning process in any subject and at any level.

In emphasizing its value as a tool for teaching substantive material and its power as a way of thinking, there's a danger that one other important attribute will be overlooked. Metaphorical thinking is *fun,* not just effective. Teachers who have used it report that students enjoy metaphorical lessons and are stimulated by them. In a highly verbal, logical style of education there is little room for mental play, yet we know that the ability to play with ideas and concepts is basic to problem solving and creativity. Metaphor allows this type of play to occur as part of the learning process, and even nonacademically oriented students respond to its appeal. A group of elementary school teachers who used some simple connection-making lessons with their classes reported: "Their eyes danced," "They had fun with it and so did I," "I saw a different side of some children; they sparkled."

SOLUTIONS TO
QUESTIONS ON PAGE 57

1. What animal is like the right hemisphere? Why? How is it different? What animal is like the left hemisphere? Why? How is it different?
   a. An *eagle* is like the right hemisphere because it gets the whole picture when it's flying. It's also very visual; it gets most of its

information through its eyes. It's different in that it can see images, but it can't create them like an artist can.

An *ant* is like the left hemisphere. It sees only features, one after another, as it moves along in a line from one place to the next. The difference is that the ant is a slave to unthinking instinct while the left hemisphere is a source of sophisticated thought.

b. A *bird* hunting for worms is like the right hemisphere: It uses all its senses; it imagines the worm under the ground.

An *ant* moving grains of food, one by one, in a line is like the left hemisphere. It's very organized, very linear. It's different because it's not logical.

Notice that the first two responses seem very similar in terms of the animals chosen, but when we look at the reasons for the choices, we find that the connections being made were quite different. The first respondent was most interested in the distinction between gestalt or holistic perception and feature detection while the second was thinking of sensory, especially visuo-spatial, thinking as opposed to a linear process. One answer is not better than the other; each offers connections which are useful.

c. A *porpoise or other sea mammal* is like the right hemisphere because of its fluidity, its greater freedom of movement. It's different because it's not very visual; it relies more on its auditory sense.

A *horse or other land mammal* is like the left hemisphere because it is more constrained by the terrain, more linear. It's different because it isn't really logical.

2. If your school were a person, what would be its right hemisphere? What would be its left hemisphere? Why?

a. Its left hemisphere would be the clock and bell system because it's temporal and linear. The right would be the physical layout of rooms because it's spatial.

b. The right hemisphere would be the campus; that's the whole, the spatial gestalt. The left would be the rooms, wiring, plumbing; they're the parts that are laid out linearly.

c. The right hemisphere would be the kids because most of them are more visual than verbal. They'd rather move around than sit in rows and listen. They prefer doing to studying. The left would be us, the faculty, because as a whole we're pretty verbal, and we have a linear idea of school with graduation as the goal at the end.

3. The relationship between the right and left hemispheres is like the one between _____ and _____ because _____

a. The relationship between the right and left hemispheres is like the one between a map and written directions on how to find a place because a map utilizes visuo-spatial abilities while the written directions depend on verbal skills.

b. The relationship between the right and left hemispheres is like the one between an artist and an engineer living next door to each other because they seem very different, but if they communicate and cooperate their relationship can be very exciting and mutually beneficial.
c. The relationship between the right and left hemispheres is like the one between night and day because together they produce dawn and twilight.

These answers are not as complete as you'd want students' responses to be because they do not make explicit their connections. The problem is especially clear in the last response. How is the way in which day and night make dawn and twilight like the relationship between the two hemispheres? There are a number of possible connections; the only way to know what the student is thinking is to ask that the connections be explained.

NOTES

1. The approach to using metaphor presented in this chapter is drawn from the work of WILLIAM J. J. GORDON and TONY POZE of Synectics Education Systems (SES). A list of books by Gordon and Poze—both texts and teaching materials—is provided in the "Metaphor" section of the Bibliography.
2. SES refers to this process as *essence identification*. Directions for deriving an essence in a problem-solving setting are found in GORDON and POZE, *The Art of the Possible* (Cambridge, Mass.: Porpoise Books, 1976), pp. 63–68.
3. For further information on the Title I project, see GORDON and POZE, "Learning Dysfunction and Connection Making," *Psychiatric Annals*, 8, no. 3 (March 1978) and GORDON, "Connection Making Is Universal," *Curriculum Product Review*, 9, No. 4 (April 1977).
4. JACQUES JIMENEZ, "Synectics: A Technique for Creative Learning," *The Science Teacher* (March 1975), p. 34.
5. GORDON and POZE, *From the Inside* (Cambridge, Mass.: Porpoise Books, 1974), pp. 76–80.
6. The lessons are from GORDON, *Making It Strange, Book IV* (New York: Harper & Row, Pub., 1969). The student's writ-

ing is quoted in GORDON, *The Metaphorical Way of Learning and Knowing,* 2nd ed. (Cambridge, Mass.: Porpoise Books, 1973), p. 112.

7. For directions on writing stretching exercises, see GORDON and POZE, *Teaching Is Listening* (Cambridge, Mass.: Porpoise Books, 1972), pp. 29–37.

8. GORDON and POZE, *Strange and Familiar, Book VI* (Cambridge, Mass.: Porpoise Books, 1972), p. 50.

9. Questions 2, 3, and 4 are taken from GORDON, *Making It Strange, Book IV.*

10. Questions 5 and 6 were written by PATRICIA ROB of Mt. Greylock Regional High School, Williamstown, Mass.

11. From ANNE RICE, "Women Writers at Work," a lecture series presented by the University of California Extension, Berkeley, November 1979.

12. GORDON and POZE, *Strange and Familiar, Book VI,* pp. 67–76.

13. GORDON and POZE, "Learning Dysfunction."

14. Ibid.

15. GORDON and POZE, *Teaching Is Listening,* pp. 14, 72–73.

VISUAL
THINKING

An architect sketches the plans for a house, a scientist squints through the eyepiece of a microscope, a poet conjures the images of a spring from her youth. All are using visual thinking, yet it's unlikely that any received training in it during the first twelve years of their schooling. Visual thinking is too often associated with the visual arts and relegated to a single area in the curriculum; yet it is a part of every subject because it is a basic way of obtaining, processing, and representing information. To ignore its role in any subject is to fail to train students in its use and to deny to those who are primarily visual processors the opportunity to learn in the mode which comes most easily for them.

The role of visual thinking in the classroom is threefold. It begins with *seeing*. Observation is a basic means of gathering and interpreting information in most fields. Whether students are in a science class observing an experiment, in a vocational education course learning to use a machine or tool, or in a math class studying geometric figures, they need to learn what to look for and how to interpret what they see. Next they need help in *representing information graphically*. Some information, such as the relationship between supply and demand in economics, the design for a building, and the structure of the digestive system, is better represented by drawings and diagrams than by verbal descriptions. Teaching students to understand and use graphic representations provides them with a tool that improves comprehension and enables them to clarify their thinking and to communicate their ideas to others. Finally, students need help developing their inner eye. *Visualizing,* the ability to generate and manipulate visual imagery, helps with a wide variety of tasks including remembering information, learning spelling words, performing mathematical functions, and solving practical problems involving spatial relations. These three uses of visual thinking will be discussed in detail later in this chapter.

When a teacher presents information both verbally and visually, students who are primarily visual processors have a much better chance of succeeding in the class. They benefit from being offered information in their strongest modality, but there is also benefit for the very verbal students even though they may resist activities that require drawing and other forms of visual representation. Such students need to be challenged to develop their visual abilities; if they are allowed to rely too much on their verbal capacity, they will not develop its visual complement. While they may be quite successful in school, they will nevertheless be deficient in a thinking skill that is important in all areas of life.

You need not be a strong visual thinker to be a visual teacher. In fact, a highly verbal teacher who is excited about rediscovering his visual capabilities can provide a powerful model for students to explore and expand their own visual thinking. The willingness to try new ways of doing things, to learn from failure as well as success, and to share one's enthusiasm for new experiences and ideas is all that's required.

TRAINING PERCEPTION

Visual perception is an important part of most subjects taught in school. The sciences and social sciences are based on observation; mathematics involves perception of relationships which can often

be represented visually. And such subjects as vocational education, cooking, and athletics require that students know what to
look for and how to interpret what they see. We tend to assume
that as long as we have 20/20 vision our visual perception is
adequate; yet if you observe students in an art class or a science
laboratory, you'll discover that there is a wide range of perceptual
skill. In *Drawing on the Right Side of the Brain,* Betty Edwards
argues that the problem with most adult and adolescent drawings
is that the left hemisphere's labels and definitions interfere with
the right hemisphere's ability to see the thing as it actually
appears.

> [to draw a cube] the child must draw the oddly angled shapes
> just as they appear—that is, just like the image that falls on
> the retina of the perceiving eye. *Those shapes are not square.*
> In fact, the child must suppress *knowing* that the cube is
> square and draw shapes that are "funny." The drawn cube
> will look like a cube *only* if it is comprised of oddly angled
> shapes. Put another way, the child must draw *unsquare*
> shapes to draw a square cube. The child must accept this
> paradox, this illogical process, which conflicts with verbal,
> conceptual knowledge.
>   . . . adult students beginning in art generally do not
> really see *what is in front of their eyes. . . .* They . . . take
> note of what's there, and quickly translate the perception
> into words and symbols mainly based on the symbol system
> developed throughout childhood and on what they *know*
> about the perceived object.[1]

One of the purposes of school is to give students experience
through which to develop and refine their observational abilities.
We direct them to look through a microscope or to observe a
chemistry or physics experiment, but we seldom train them in the
process of observation. Too often the purpose of the exercise is to
demonstrate a principle from the book. It may help students remember the information for a while, but it does not teach them
how to discover information for themselves. Some students will
teach themselves to make meaning from the shapes on the microscope slide; others will stare intently through the eyepiece hoping
desperately for insight and achieving only eyestrain. We need to
place at least as much emphasis on the processes of observation as
on the principles that experiments are designed to teach.

Before reading any further, take a few moments to consider what you do to train visual perception through your teaching.

EXERCISE 1

What visual sources of information do you provide?
　　　How do you train perception?
　　　How do you help students learn what to look for and how to interpret what they see (for example, what signs tell you a cake is done or a tooth comes from a herbivore or a group of people believe in an afterlife)?
　　　How do you evaluate visual perception periodically to determine which students are having difficulty with it?

Drawing.　　One of the best ways to train observation skills is to ask students to draw what they see. Drawing requires that one look carefully and observe both details and overall spatial relationships. Frequently, the act of drawing makes one aware of features that were missed by a more casual examination. As Ross Parmenter explains,

> In addition to leading to exact observing of parts . . . drawing . . . enforces complete observing of wholes. This is compelled by the curious way a gap in a drawing shows up much more vividly than a gap in one's seeing. Our habit of seeing sketchily is so strong, and generally so unrecognized, that when we look at an object we will not be aware of its parts that are not registering. But when you work on a drawing you are forced to study that part of the model which you did not realize had to be in the picture.[2]

In addition a drawing is a visual representation of what the student has seen; it can provide insight into how she perceives the things she is drawing. Does she leave things out? What is emphasized, what ignored? If she's missed something, you can point to the spot on the drawing where it should be and ask her to look again and see what goes there. If she still can't distinguish a detail, draw it in and ask her to find it on the thing being drawn. Working closely with students' drawings, you can learn how they observe and train them to overcome deficits.

Many older students and not a few teachers will avoid drawing because they associate it with artistic skill and feel insecure in their abilities. One need not be a poet or novelist to write the English language and use it to communicate effectively. By the same token, one need not be an artist to draw. Kimon Nicolaides' description of drawing helps put it in perspective as a tool of thinking.

> It has nothing to do with artifice or technique. It has nothing to do with aesthetics or conception. It has only to do with the act of correct observation, and by that I mean a physical contact with all sorts of objects through all the senses.[3]

Recognizing the value of drawing as a thinking tool opens the way for new cooperation between art teachers and other members of the faculty. Think of how the curriculum would be enriched if students could take a team-taught course in drawing and writing, if every week the biology class spent one period with the art teacher learning to draw the life forms they were studying, if history included the study of the art of the time along with the events.

Even if you are unable to arrange for an art teacher to work with your students to develop drawing skills, do not let that prevent you from encouraging students to draw. Stress that you are concerned with seeing, not drawing, and that the process of producing the sketch is more important than the appearance of the final product. Reward students for making the effort (which for poor drawers may be considerable), not on the quality of the image.

Verbal Description.   Just as drawing can sharpen and improve observation skills, verbal description can also contribute. Robert McKim describes the process:

> Because much knowledge is most usually stored in relation to language, words can powerfully catalyze seeing. Scientific observers are especially alert to the way careful verbal description brings knowledge to play and thereby makes seeing more accurate.
>
> Not any sort of language will do, however. Cliché label-

ing leads only to cliché seeing. As Parmenter puts it, "Don't chip away at things to make them fit words, but instead conscientiously use words to try to make them fit things." Such a search for precise verbal description does three things: (1) it enhances visual memory by relating visual imagery to existing verbal knowledge, (2) it disciplines seeing by joining verbal and visual searching together, and (3) it educates ambidextrous thinking.[4]

The impact of verbal description on seeing is not limited to science. One of the hallmarks of outstanding writing is its ability to affect the way the reader sees the world. A particularly powerful prose passage or poem creates mental images which help the reader to look again at familiar surroundings with new awareness and appreciation.

In helping students put words to their observations, it's important to distinguish between labeling and description: Each has its place in the classroom. Often, applying the appropriate label does not require close observation. Parmenter notes that:

a thing that has been given a name tends to lose its particularity. And because particularity is precious, names that merely embody concepts or denote functions can be like cloaks of invisibility. Drawing, however, emphasizes and helps to preserve particularity.[5]

If you want students to observe carefully, you'll need to phrase your directions to exclude labels. "Look at the slide and describe exactly what you see so carefully that you can later recognize the structures from your descriptions of them" is much more likely to train observation skills than a simple directive to find and label X, Y, and Z.

History teachers may object that theirs is a subject in which visual perception plays little or no role. The fact that visual material is seldom included is less a statement on its value than on the teaching of the subject. In history and social studies, students are often asked to study people and places without having much sense of what they look like. For most students but especially for those who are highly visual, it's very difficult to be interested in a place or culture that one hasn't seen. Verbal description, especially the kind found in most textbooks, is not sufficient to create vivid mental images. Without those images, learning is reduced to the manipulation of information—memorizing the important facts and statistics and drawing correct conclusions. One may write an essay or answer a set of questions on nomads with no real idea of where or how they live or why it is worth studying them.

The illustrations and photographs in textbooks are rarely sufficient to create a sense of place. Fortunately, photo essays have become a popular and expanding area in book publishing, so most libraries contain beautiful large books of photographs on various peoples and places. These books provide an aesthetic as well as a learning experience.

Films also provide a valuable source of visual information. Unfortunately, in most films the narration functions like a text, telling students what they are supposed to learn and encouraging them to use their ears instead of their eyes to gather information. It is often useful to turn the sound track off and have students watch in silence. In some cases it is also useful to have students view a film more than once. If you turn off the sound track, students are likely to have questions which can be discussed and then resolved by a second viewing.

Simply showing a film or making pictures available is no guarantee that students will make use of them as learning tools. Many students look upon movies as a pleasant diversion requiring no thought or effort on their part. They must be educated to extract information from a visual medium just as they've been taught (hopefully) to find it in a verbal presentation. Before you show a film or give out a book, give them guidelines of what to look for. You can ask questions and require that they support conclusions with evidence from the photos or film ("What's the climate like?" "It's hot." "What did you see that convinced you of that?" "The people didn't wear many clothes and there were lots of palm trees."). Training students to be skilled observers is just as important as training them to be careful readers. Essential mental skills such as classifying, generalizing, and abstracting can all be developed with visual materials as well as with verbal ones.

Even in English, that most verbal of subjects, there is a place for observation. The writer, whether poet, novelist, or essayist, must be an astute observer. The difference between good descriptive writing and mediocre writing is often the writer's ability to make us see the world through a new, sharper perspective. Stereotyped or superficial perception is reflected in stereotyped, superficial writing.

GRAPHIC REPRESENTATION

Information can be recorded and represented in a number of ways. The most common way in our society is written language, but it is not always the best, and by itself it is not nearly as effective as when it is supplemented with a graphic representation of the same information.

Drawing is usually thought of as representative—that is, it's supposed to look like something. Drawing as we'll consider it in this chapter is a much broader form of expression and is rarely representative. It is more apt to be a rough diagram drawn to illustrate a point or a cluster map made to organize a paper. Its purpose most often is to communicate concepts or to serve as a thinking tool, a way of capturing half-formed thoughts and ideas and working with them to discover meaning. This use of drawing requires little or no artistic skill and is well within the capabilities of even the poorest drawer.

There are two main areas a teacher needs to consider in integrating visual representation into classroom activities. These are (1) presenting and clarifying ideas graphically, and (2) teaching students to interpret and use graphic representation. Most of the time a teacher's use of graphic images is for the purpose of presenting and clarifying ideas and concepts. Since such images are learning tools, they should represent careful thinking about the subject. They need not be polished or beautiful, but they should be clear.

Student drawings, on the other hand, often represent attempts to understand the subject. They may be incomplete or inaccurate; errors should be seen as a means of discovering where a student needs help. If students feel their drawings must be perfect, they will not use them when they need them most—that is, in cases where they are unclear about the subject. Therefore, except in cases where drawing is part of a test, it should be used as a learning tool. Errors should be greeted with, "Ah, this helps me see where the problem is," not "That's wrong."

There are a number of techniques for graphic representation—key words, diagrams, charts, graphs, maps, cluster maps, idea sketches, mandalas, cartoons, expressive drawings, and constructions. Each has its value for representing information of a particular sort, and the use of each one extends and expands its maker's viewpoint. As Bob McKim points out,

> Every graphic expression embodies a viewpoint, a single way of looking at reality; by encoding an idea in a variety of graphic languages, the visual thinker represents the idea more completely. . . . every time the thinker changes graphic languages, he submits his idea to a new set of built-in mental operations.[6]

Whether you use visual representation a great deal or very seldom, it's useful to become aware of exactly the role it plays in your class. The following exercise will help you do this.

EXERCISE 2

For the next two weeks keep track of your use of graphic representation. Begin with your blackboard, overhead projector transparencies, or wherever else you write or draw for students to see. At the end of each lesson, look at your blackboard or transparencies as the visual record of that lesson. Do they communicate the material you wanted to teach? Is the most important information represented in some way? If not, in your next lesson plans, include explicit plans for noting key words and concepts on the board and for representing major points and ideas in a visual form.

Key Words. Spoken language can, for some students, become a stream of sound, as difficult to decipher as a foreign language. If the subject is unfamiliar or the student is insecure in it, this problem is even more apt to occur. To help students organize their listening and focus their attention on what's important, you can use the simple technique of key words. As you introduce an important concept or piece of information, write it clearly on the board. The words focus attention, organize information, and reinforce the spoken presentation. Seeing the written words will actually aid some students in remembering what you've said. It also helps students identify what you consider major points to be understood.

Organizing key words into a mind map or cluster map (a technique described later in this chapter) provides an even more useful record. The map places concepts in relation to each other, making clear which ideas are primary, which secondary, and so forth. It enables students to *see* the concepts you've covered displayed in a coherent nonlinear form of organization, offering them at the same time a sense of the whole and of the significant parts.

Charting, Diagraming, and Graphing. These techniques produce images that vary from a mathematical graph to a freeform diagram like Figure 3.2 on page 49. Their common quality is their ability to express relationships visually. Math and science teachers tend to use graphs and charts more than other teachers because their subject requires the perception of relationships which can be represented numerically and graphically. However, any subject can be illustrated with rough sketches that represent ideas.

The diagram in Figure 3.2 is an example of such a drawing. It is the type of sketch one might put on the board to illustrate a point while teaching. It lacks the exactness of a graph; its lines have no numerical value. Its purpose is to represent the information about learning styles in a visual manner in order to clarify the concept. Such diagrams reinforce a point for those who already understand it and provide additional help for those who have difficulty with the verbal explanation.

While charts and graphs are a part of the curriculum in many math courses, students often perceive them as information to be learned rather than tools to be used. This attitude is encouraged when the teacher's use of graphs and charts is restricted to units dealing explicitly with those subjects. If students see charts used as a tool to solve other kinds of problems, they are more likely to use them in their own efforts to solve problems.

Andrew Williams, who teaches economics at the University of California, encourages his students to translate verbal information into graphs by reminding them to "draw the picture." Each time he presents a concept, he asks, "What do we do now?" He reports that before long the students automatically respond, "Draw the picture." This type of explicit teaching makes graphs less intimidating to students and trains them to use graphs as a way to understand the subject.

Franette Walberg, a resource teacher in the Acalanes Union High School District in California, teaches students to use charting and diagraming to organize information so that they can solve word problems in math. She encourages them to picture the information in the problem and to represent it visually. Look at Problem 1. To solve it you must be clear on the relationships. You could write them out or put them in the form of an equation, but for most of us the simplest and clearest way to represent this information is visually, in the form of a diagram. Problem 2, though it is a different type of problem, can also be represented with a diagram. Figure 5.1 shows the diagrams that represent the verbal information from each problem. Ms. Walberg's excellent book, *Puzzle Thinking,* includes many ways of teaching students to use visual strategies to solve math problems and think logically.

PROBLEM 1

Paul and Ben are both older than John. Laurie is younger than Paul, but older than Ben. Mary is older than Paul. Who is youngest and who is next to youngest?

PROBLEM 2

It is 90 miles from Hartford to Milltown. Anne's car ran out of gas halfway through the second third of the trip. How many more miles does she need to go to reach Milltown?

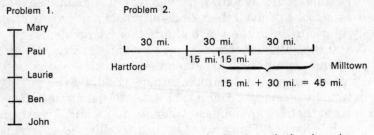

Figure 5.1 Problems 1 and 2 can be solved more easily if students draw diagrams to represent the information.

Time Lines. A time line is a form of linear diagram that displays the sequence of events over time. It is particularly useful in history, where students are faced with a great deal of information and may have difficulty making meaning of it. The time line provides a "picture" of a period which gives them an overview, a sense of the whole that integrates the facts and dates they have learned. The simplest form of time line is a continuum on which events are entered next to their dates. However, it is important to realize that simply entering a string of events on a time line does not endow them with meaning. It helps in clarifying their sequence and is a useful quick reference, but it does not accomplish much more than that.

A more complex and potentially powerful time line can be constructed by entering events and movements in categories established along the vertical axis. Figure 5.2 is an example of one such time line. It enables one to represent not only events of political importance but also movements and discoveries in philosophy, religion, art, science, and technology. One can choose any set of categories; for example, to represent the rise of imperialism, one could place the names of countries or areas of the world along the vertical axis and enter events related to imperialism under the countries affected. The categories selected will depend on the period and the focus of study. Using different colors for each category will make the time line clearer and easier to interpret.

As with the other techniques in this book, the value of time lines is greatly increased when students are asked to generate their own product rather than to copy or study the teacher's. The

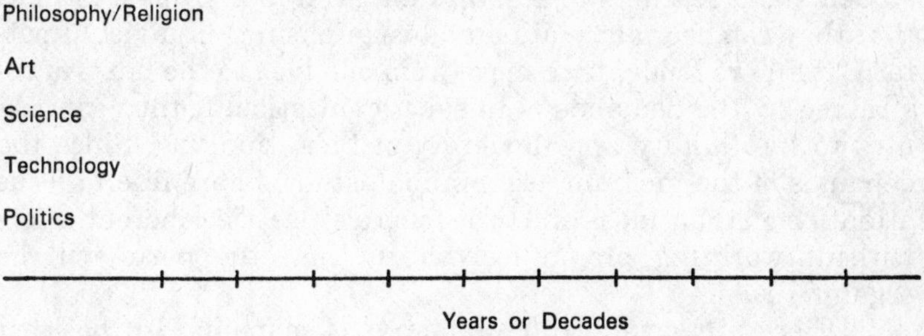

Philosophy/Religion

Art

Science

Technology

Politics

Years or Decades

Figure 5.2   A time line can show events in different areas simultaneously. The dates are entered along the line at measured distances so each year or decade gets equal space; and important events, discoveries, movements, and so on are placed in appropriate places.

process of designing one's own time line requires decisions on how to represent a period most clearly and completely, what categories to use, and which events belong under which categories. In the process of making those decisions, students are required to analyze and study the period being covered, and they are much more likely to remember the material.

Time lines can be used in other subjects as well. Mary Frances Claggett, who teaches writing at Alameda High School, in Alameda, California, has students draw a time line for their own lives, then teaches them about character development by having them create a character and draw a time line of that person's life. Such lines provide a kind of map based on time on which one can plot out major events and influences and develop the sense of a whole character, thus avoiding the kind of stereotyping that often mars student writing.

Mapping.   For many years outlining has been taught as the standard way of organizing material for a written or oral presentation and of representing information from books and lectures. Outlines are quintessentially linear forms. For students whose minds are not particularly linear, being required to represent information linearly demands tremendous effort and may actually detract from their learning and destroy any interest or excitement about the topic.

Mapping offers a happy alternative to outlining. It enables

97

students and teachers to organize material in a graphic form so
that they can see information and relationships in a visual pattern. It allows students to move from one idea to the next, unre-
strained by the demands of linear organization; it thus contributes to the fluidity and flexibility of their thinking. Since the
demands of the medium are minimal, students are free to focus
attention on their ideas and to develop a sense of a coherent whole
without worrying prematurely about how the parts will be
organized.

There are several different ways of mapping. In the least
structured form, which we'll call *clustering* (Figure 5.3), the central idea is placed in the center of the paper and circled. Other
ideas are arranged around that idea with arrows indicating how
one point leads into the next. In a more structured form, which
we'll call *mapping* (Figure 5.4), the main theme is placed in the
center of the page and secondary points are represented on lines
branching out from the center with their own branches carrying
supporting information. A pattern is formed in which an idea's
importance is clearly displayed by its proximity to the center. In
both cases, since the presentation is graphic, information is dis-
tilled into key words, phrases, or images.

Mary Frances Claggett and Gabriele Rico of the University
of California Bay Area Writing Project use clustering to teach
writing. They point out that while writing is a verbal activity, the
process of writing involves both right- and left-hemisphere thinking. In the prewriting phase of composing, too much attention to
detail or sequence can block the flow of ideas. In this phase the
writer needs to generate ideas freely and allow them to suggest
their own structure, to shut off the logical, sequential judgments
of the left hemisphere in order to shape a coherent whole. Rico
and Claggett maintain that when writing assignments are preceded by clustering the results are increased fluency and co-
herence, greater use of specific detail, a more sophisticated sense
of how to develop and expand ideas, and increased use of mature
sentence patterns.[7] Figure 5.3 shows a student cluster and the
writing derived from it.

In *Use Both Sides of Your Brain,* Tony Buzan presents a
form of mapping which he calls *mind mapping.* He places all

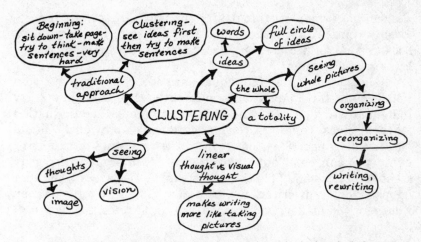

Figure 5.3 This cluster diagram was done by a student who had studied clustering in a writing class. Here is a part of the paper she wrote from the map.

"Clustering helps make writing for me more like taking a picture. It gives me the opportunity to see the whole before trying to tackle a part, or to see a part before trying to tackle the whole.

When I first started school, the idea of having to write was frightening. Now I look forward to writing and do it more and more. I still have a lot of mechanical problems, but I enjoy writing, and putting thoughts on paper helps to clarify them in my mind. . . . Once I see the end—the point or main focus—I know better what to put in the middle and beginning to provide an even flow of thoughts." (Sharon Hall in Gabriele Lusser Rico and Mary Frances Claggett, *Balancing the Hemispheres: Brain Research and the Teaching of Writing* (Berkeley, Ca.: Bay Area Writing Project, University of California, Berkeley, 1980), pp. 34–35.)

words on lines and requires that each line be connected to at least one other line to guarantee that the pattern has basic structure. Buzan suggests that mapping is a basic study skill which can be used to take notes on textbooks or lectures, to review and remember information, to plan, and to solve problems. Mapping, like clustering, can be used to plan a writing assignment. In fact, most of the chapters of this book began as maps. In many cases, their use shortened the planning process from several days to a few hours.

The pattern of a map allows one to see and represent connections more easily than does a linear outline. A number of simple devices can be used. They include arrows, colors, geometric

shapes (for example, triangles might mark the connection between events in an author's life and themes in his works on a
book report), and codes, such as asterisks, exclamation points,
crosses, and numbers.[8]

Maps are a highly individual form of representing information. One of their advantages over outlines is that they allow
individuals to determine the best way to represent information
for themselves. Therefore, the guidelines given previously should
be used as suggestions, not rules. In commenting on students'
maps, you can point out where their style of organization may
create problems and help them be aware of the causes when that
happens, but your criterion should always be how well the map
works for the maker, not an arbitrary set of rules.

Figure 5.4   This map is used to summarize the discussion of mapping in Marilyn
Hanf Buckley and Owen Boyle, *Mapping the Writing Journey* (Berkeley, Calif.: Bay
Area Writing Project, Tolman Hall, University of California, Berkeley, 1981), p. 36.

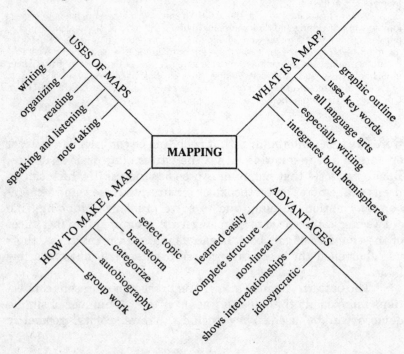

Mandalas. Just as mapping provides a visual pattern which unifies separate parts into a whole, the mandala creates meaning within a circular pattern. The mandala is an archetypal shape. Rhoda Kellogg has found the circle with a cross inside it in children's drawings from every culture she's studied.[9] This ancient form plays a prominent part in artistic and religious expression, especially in Eastern cultures.

There are no rules or formulas for constructing mandalas. One approach is to ask students to develop a series of images and arrange them within a circle. Another technique is to divide the circle into halves, quarters, or pie-shaped sections and put images for different ideas or concepts in each section. The circle can also be divided into one or more concentric circles which represent different levels of an idea. If the mandala represents a central theme or concept, an image for the concept should be placed at the center of the circle. For examples of specific mandala assignments connected with writing, see Rico and Claggett, *Balancing the Hemispheres.*[10]

Mandalas can be used in any subject; for example, in civics courses the three branches of government are often represented by an organization chart. The same relationships can be placed within a circle divided into thirds. The constraints of the form will stimulate original thinking, and the final product will have dynamic aesthetic dimensions that a chart lacks. Figure 1.1 and Figure 10.1 are mandalas used to express a concept.

Mary Frances Claggett uses mandalas as a form for studying literature. Students are asked to select a number of images which express what they feel to be the important themes or ideas in a book and to arrange them within the circle to make a statement about the book. The visual statement may stand on its own or form the basis for a poem or essay.

As with any technique, it's best to start with tasks that are simple until you've gained confidence. In introducing mandalas to students do not ask for complex, elaborate drawings with many parts. A simple mandala can be as elegant and satisfying as a more complex one, and it will not overwhelm a beginner.

Cartooning. You need not be Charles Schulz (creator of *Peanuts*) to use cartooning. Anyone can master stick figures, and their use

Figure 5.5   This mandala was drawn by Maureen Chambers, a sophomore in Genie Miller's humanities class at Albany High School in Albany, Calif. After looking at a variety of mandalas, students were asked to select a number of images that represented themselves and to create their own personal mandalas using those images.

allows you to communicate many ideas more effectively. Figure 5.6 is a cartoon Gene Davis of Albany High School uses to explain diffusion across a membrane (the movement of particles from an area of high density to an area of low density). Mr. Davis names his figures after students in the class, usually the biggest boy and the smallest girl, and tells the class that the two hate each other. He explains that the fence is the membrane and points out that since Laura has all the bricks, she can move more bricks initially to Tim's side of the fence. However, Tim, being no fool, will begin to throw Laura's bricks back. When the same number of bricks are moving in both directions, there is an *equilibrium*. Mr. Davis illustrates the effect of energy change on diffusion rates and equilibrium shifts by pointing out that the most energetic thrower can change the rate of exchange (Tim can throw faster, or Laura can enlist Keiko to help throw bricks).

If you want to get a little fancier with your stick figures, a basic book on cartooning will help you. *The Big Yellow Drawing Book* by Dan, Marian, and Hugh O'Neill Jr. is an excellent introduction to both cartooning and drawing, created specifically for teachers and students. You'll find it listed in the "Visual Thinking" section of the Bibliography. But remember that a crude cartoon is better than no cartoon.

Figure 5.6

Idea Sketches.   An idea sketch can be a diagram, chart, map, cluster map, or drawing. It is defined not by its form but by its purpose as a tool of thinking. Idea sketches are the graphic representation of the mind at work. They are usually rough sketches which may not be comprehensible to anyone but the maker. The process of producing the sketch is more important than the sketch itself because in figuring out how to represent a concept graphically, the maker extends his understanding of it. Moving from the verbal statement of an idea to a visual representation requires one to think about that idea in a new way, to consider elements that may not have suggested themselves before, to discover new possibilities. The result is usually increased understanding and insight. Choose one of the following exercises to give you some experience with this type of translation from one medium to another.

EXERCISE 3

Select a concept you are planning to teach that you usually explain verbally (don't use one you illustrate with diagrams). Now draw or diagram the concept. Don't worry about whether anyone else will understand your work, and don't think about what you'll draw before you begin drawing. You may use words as labels.

EXERCISE 4

Write a paragraph or two describing your teaching style. Now take a blank sheet of paper and sketch your teaching style in whatever manner suggests itself to you. You may use images to create a picture, or you may construct a map or diagram. You may use words as labels.

Idea sketches are a personal tool; their purpose is to clarify thinking, not to communicate it to others. However, such sketches can be used to help you determine when a student is confused and needs additional help. When a student is having trouble understanding an idea or concept, you can ask him to draw it, as he understands it, then use the idea sketch as a way of clarifying the concept. Have him explain his sketch as he draws it since it is not the sketch that is important but the thinking that produced it. Visual thinkers may be much better at drawing their ideas than putting them into words; with their drawing to work from, it may be easier for them to verbalize their understanding and for you to discover and then to explain the points that are creating difficulty. You can see this technique with any subject. For example,

Science: Draw what you think the process/structure/system looks like.

History: Show me what the period would look like if you made a map of it. Draw the power relations.

English: If you put that concept in the form of a diagram or idea sketch, what would it look like?

Expressive Drawing, Constructions, and Other Art Activities. Elementary school teachers frequently reinforce lessons by having students draw about what they've learned. Students draw plants growing from seeds, volcanoes erupting, events from books they've read, and even math problems. History or social studies lessons are often supplemented with activities which give the students experiences that make the lessons more meaningful. They may draw or construct a model of an Indian village or make Polynesian designs on cloth, weave a basket, or make a cornhusk doll. These experiences, while providing pleasure and motivation, also increase understanding and connect information with experience.

Unfortunately, as children become older, art activities are separated from their studies and relegated to separate art classes which often focus on technique and may intimidate the less artistically gifted child. Yet art can be an effective part of any subject at any age level.

At Walden School in Berkeley, California, teachers coordinate their second- through fourth-grade art and writing classes so that students may write a myth in one class and make a wire or clay sculpture of a character from it in the other class. They've found that some students find the writing easier if they've begun with the spatial representation; others need to begin with words. Sometimes they work in two dimensions as in painting, sometimes in three dimensions as in sculpting; some activities are done individually, some by the group, as when a group myth becomes a group mural. The greater the variety of activities, the more opportunity students have to discover their strengths and to gain practice to overcome their weaknesses.

In a high school English class studying *The Tempest*, Anne Villalon of Mt. Greylock High School in Williamstown, Massachusetts, offers students the choice of drawing or writing a description of two characters—Caliban and Ariel. When they finish, they present their work and discuss the characters in terms of it. Then she asks the artists to write and the writers to draw the characters. They discuss how the experiences are different and consider drawing and writing both as thinking and communication tools and as part of each student's personal style.

Genie Miller of Albany High School, Albany, California, includes art projects as part of her history courses to help students understand different aspects of the life and culture of each period. In medieval history, she asks them to draw a cathedral floor plan, to illuminate a page of manuscript, and to create a geometric design like the ones used in Moslem art. The projects not only stimulate involvement and enthusiasm; they also provide an additional avenue for understanding basic concepts. When students compare a mosque with a cathedral or Moslem patterns with Christian illustrations of Biblical scenes, they discover a concrete, visual representation of the differences between the two world views.

Projects involving expressive drawings, constructions, or collages are within every teacher's capability. However, they can provide even richer experience if children also receive instruction in art. One need only compare the quality of the pictures made by children from Waldorf schools, where art is an important part of the curriculum, with pictures from public schools to realize how much children miss by the exclusion of art instruction. The children in Waldorf schools learn the basic skills of using different materials to produce highly original and beautiful works of art; they are able to use these skills in every academic subject. Their diagrams of biological systems and their illustrations of history or writing assignments have an elegance that is astonishing to teachers unfamiliar with Waldorf techniques. All children have the capacity to produce this beauty; when we fail to give them instruction and materials, we deny them an important area of experience which could produce greater involvement in all subjects and bolster their self-esteem.

Using Color. Color is an important tool in visual thinking. It separates ideas so they can be seen more easily; it stimulates creativity and aids the memory. Color captures and directs attention. Even conventionally outlined notes can benefit from color coding; maps, cluster maps, mandalas, and most expressive drawings are considerably more effective in color.

In teaching writing, Mary Frances Claggett of Alameda High School, Alameda, California, makes students more aware of their use of language and structures the revision of their first drafts by asking them to underline certain parts of speech in one color and others in another. When working on concrete and abstract language, she has students underline concrete nouns in one color and abstract nouns in another. They then have a visual picture of the concentration and distribution of each type of noun. As part of their revision, she instructs them to change all abstract nouns to concrete ones. In another assignment she tells students to underline (1) all verbs in one color, (2) all *to be* verbs in a second color, and (3) all passive verbs in a third. Then she tells them to eliminate the *to be* verbs and to change the passive verbs to active. In these assignments, color helps shape the revision process, directing the students' attention to specific points where changes are required.

Having students use pens of four different colors to do a task can give you information on the way they approach it. Neuropsychologists give students four pens and have them work with each pen in a specific order for a specified period of time (red pen for three minutes, then blue for three minutes, and so on). The results reveal a good deal about how the child did the task, what was done first, second, or third. You can use this technique on math problems, writing, drawing a diagram, or taking notes. It

will tell you how different children approach the task, how they
handle revision or checking, whether they produce more at the
beginning or the end of an assignment, and where they tend to
make errors.[11]

If you haven't used color much in your teaching, get a box of
colored chalk and see what possibilities it opens for you. Ask
students to bring colored pens to class and experiment with ways
of using them. At first, it may seem artificial and cumbersome to
make conscious use of color; after all, you will be changing your
basic pattern of representing information. However, as with any
new tool, if you will make the initial effort, it will become easier
with time, and you will discover that it offers new possibilities.

VISUALIZATION

Visualization, the ability to recall and construct visual images
within the mind, is so basic a thinking mode that it is difficult to
include all its uses in a single chapter. For this reason, we'll make
a distinction between visualization and fantasy, and treat fantasy
in Chapter 6. In this chapter, visualization will be discussed in
terms of an arbitrarily assigned definition of inner imagery that
is fairly static. Fantasy is like a multisensory movie; the type of
imagery we'll discuss in this chapter is more like still photos. One
may manipulate and transform these inner images, but they are
not part of an unfolding story as they would be in a fantasy.

You had an opportunity to test your own powers of visualization in several of the exercises in Chapter 3, and the problems
in that chapter should have made you aware of the uses of visualization in problem solving. Now we'll consider its role in learning.
For highly visual thinkers information is understood, manipulated, and stored in mental images. For those who can move easily between thinking modes, the use of mental imagery depends
upon the demands of the task. However, for all students, visualization can be a valuable tool for many learning tasks. We'll
consider its uses in several areas.

Reading Comprehension.   Reading comprehension is not a purely verbal process; for the written symbols to have meaning, they

must be associated with the objects, actions, and qualities they represent. Being able to decode—that is, to pronounce—a word from its written form does not guarantee comprehension. In 1973, Joel R. Levin conducted an experiment with students whose reading problems seemed associated with comprehension rather than decoding. These students were below grade level in all areas on the Iowa Test, but they scored less than one year below on the vocabulary subtest. One group of these students was told to read a story and imagine a picture for each sentence that was read. The second group read the same story but without imagining pictures. The students who visualized images to go with the sentences scored 40 percent higher on reading comprehension.[12]

"The Mind's Eye" project of Escondido, California, has also demonstrated that training students to generate mental images as they read can substantially improve reading comprehension. Teachers or aides show students how to identify key words which will help make a mental image and encourage the children to use those words to generate images. Gains in reading comprehension from this nine-week program almost tripled prior yearly average gains. Recall was twelve times greater than previous yearly gains, and while improvements in speed and accuracy were less dramatic, those scores doubled over the previous year's.[13]

Memory. Visualization has been used as an aid to memory since the ancient Greeks and probably long before that. Before we look at specific techniques for its use, take a few minutes to do the following exercise.

EXERCISE 5

Take two minutes to learn the following list of words. Then close the book and list as many as you can remember on a sheet of paper.

Lake	lemon	girl
ball	basket	jewel
cow	street	potato
moon	tree	car

Now take two minutes to learn the following words, but this time link the words in the form of a visual image. For example, in the preceding list you might have remembered girl, lake, and basket by constructing the image of a girl swimming in a lake with a basket on her head. After two minutes close the book and write the second list on a separate piece of paper.

doll	pen	bean
bag	house	mountain
fork	flower	rug
sun	dog	garage

Most people do better at remembering the second list than they did with the first. Constructing visual images associated with the words aids in recall. Though many of us decry the overemphasis on memorization in education, there are times when we want students to remember facts and information. At such times it is important to teach them a strategy for remembering. One such strategy is the "loci" method, which was developed by Simonides, a Greek poet of the fifth and sixth centuries B.C. This method was also used by Roman orators; it enabled them to remember long sequences of information so that they could speak from memory for as long as several hours without forgetting a single point.

The students were instructed to select a place they knew very well, such as their house, school, yard, or the street on which they lived. Then for each point they wished to remember they were to construct a vivid image. The first image was then placed in a given spot near the entrance of the location they'd chosen and the students visualized the image clearly in that spot against its background. The next point was represented by another image and placed in the next location; for example, the first image might be on the front door, the next in the hall, the next on the living room chair, and so on. When the exercise was finished, the students needed only to "walk" mentally through their visualized settings, seeing each image in order, and they would be reminded of the points they wished to make.

Some images are more easily remembered than others. The best images for recall should be vivid. It helps to exaggerate the image, making it very large, long, or small, and to make it funny or ridiculous (a small chair sitting on a huge plate is easier to remember than an ordinary plate on a chair). The image should be as brightly colored as possible and as dramatic. Just as humorous images are recalled more easily, so are vulgar or sexual images.

John Lane, a history teacher at Mt. Greylock High School in Williamstown, Massachusetts, teaches his students the loci method early in his course and encourages them to use it whenever he wants them to remember a sequence of events. He makes the training of memory an explicit part of the class because he feels it is basic to success in the subject.

The loci method is useful for remembering in sequence; where sequence is not important one can create images which associate or connect two or more things without putting them in a setting. You did this already in Exercise 5. In a history class a student who has difficulty remembering certain dates can imagine a historical scene and place the date in the scene.

Another application of visualization which many teachers use without being aware of it is the suggestion of visual and other sensory images as part of a verbal presentation. A skillful lecturer uses words not only to communicate ideas but to create sensory experience, to make the listener see and feel what's being discussed. There are a number of ways to cue imagery: You can use phrases such as, "If you could see this, it would look like . . . ," "I imagine this as looking . . . ," or "The image I have of that is. . . ." The cue need not always be explicit. If the words you use are evocative of sensory experience—that is, if they suggest how something looks and feels—your listeners will probably generate images to fit the words.

Figure 5.7 This cartoon is a ninth grader's image for the Boston Tea Party. He chose to use exaggeration and humor to make the image more memorable. Drawn by Alex Grishaver of the Arts Magnet School in Oakland, California.

Spelling. The staff of the Not Ltd Division of Training and Research, who use a technique they call Neuro-Linguistic Programming (NLP), have studied good spellers to determine the strategies that bring success. They maintain that the best spellers are those who can recall a stored visual image of the word. NLP theory contends that individuals' eye movements are related to and therefore reflect how they are processing information. According to the theory, most people look up and to the left when recalling information they've stored visually. NLP trainers therefore encourage people who want to remember an image to look up to the left, and they recommend that teachers place information they want stored as an image in the upper left corner of the blackboard.[14]

You can help students learn spelling words by teaching them to use visual memory. When you ask them to spell, remind them to check the "picture" and, if it's not clear, to look back at the word again. Whenever you are testing spelling, remind students to look at the picture before they write and to check the word against the picture after they write it.

Each time you put a graphic representation of an idea on the blackboard, you offer a visual image which can be stored and recalled as a means to retrieve that information. Many students, however, are unaware of the value of such images as memory aids. They need to be reminded to use them.

Gene Davis of Albany High School, Albany, California, takes a few moments before any test to do a relaxation exercise with students. As part of the exercise, he reminds them that they carry pictures of their notes and the textbook in their minds. He tells them that whenever they encounter difficulty they should breathe deeply and check their mental image file. Many students report that his technique has helped them. It is ironic that students spend so much time and energy to devise techniques to sneak information into a test when with practice they could place it in their mind's eye and have access to it at any time.

CONCLUSION

Visual thinking is so basic a part of the way we function that all of us—teachers and students—use it all the time. The value of studying its uses and of becoming aware of the role it plays in learning is that it enables us to make conscious use of a powerful tool and thus extends our effectiveness. Making visual thinking an explicit part of classroom learning also enables students to develop their capabilities in that area so that they may become more efficient learners.

NOTES

1. BETTY EDWARDS, *Drawing on the Right Side of the Brain* (Los Angeles, Calif.: J. P. Tarcher, 1979), pp. 73–74, 78.
2. ROSS PARMENTER, *The Awakened Eye* (Middletown, Conn.: Wesleyan University Press, 1968), p. 192.
3. KIMON NICOLAIDES, *The Natural Way to Draw* (Boston: Houghton Mifflin Company, 1941), p. xiii.
4. From R. H. McKIM, *Experiences in Visual Thinking* (Monterey, Calif.: Brooks/Cole, 1962), reprinted by permission of the publisher. Copyright © 1972, by Wadsworth Publishing Company.
5. PARMENTER, *The Awakened Eye,* p. 203.
6. McKIM, *Experiences in Visual Thinking,* p. 126.
7. GABRIELE LUSSER RICO and MARY FRANCES CLAGGETT, *Balancing the Hemispheres: Brain Research and the Teaching of Writing* (Berkeley, Calif.: Bay Area Writing Project, University of California, Berkeley, 1980), p. 27.
8. TONY BUZAN, *Use Both Sides of Your Brain* (New York: Dutton, 1974), p. 101.
9. RHODA KELLOGG, *Analyzing Children's Art* (Palo Alto, Calif.: Mayfield, 1969), pp. 64–69.
10. RICO and CLAGGETT, *Balancing the Hemispheres,* pp. 28–31, 58–69.
11. From PATRICIA S. DAVIDSON, "Exploring the Neuropsychology of Math," a workshop presented by the California Association of Neurologically Handicapped Children—An Association for Children and Adults with Learning Disabilities (CANHC-ACLD), San Francisco, Calif., February 1982.
12. JOEL R. LEVIN, "Inducing Comprehension in Poor Readers: A Test of a Recent Model," *Journal of Educational Psychology,* 65, no. 1 (August 1973), pp. 19–24.

13. MARJORIE PRESSLEY et al., *The Mind's Eye* (Escondido, Calif.: Escondido Union School District Board of Education, 1979).
14. *Neuro-Linguistic Programming in Education* (Santa Cruz, Calif.: Not Ltd Division of Training and Research, 1980), pp. 13–20.

∂|6

FANTASY

Gee, I fantasize a lot during class anyway.
It's exciting to find out I can use it for something.
A HIGH SCHOOL JUNIOR

Fantasizing is something that everybody does but relatively few people *use*. The distinction is an important one. It is the difference between an unwelcome visitor who chatters and distracts you and an imaginative colleague who contributes to your efforts. Since the only form of fantasy that usually gets inside a classroom is the distracting visitor, few students discover that they can use fantasy as a tool and even fewer learn how to control their imagination so that it works for them. Research in problem solving and creativity indicates that this is a serious loss since effective, creative adults make frequent use of fantasy for a number of purposes.

Fantasy is a door to our inner world, that magical realm where the imagination creates its own realities unfettered by the limitations we encounter in the outer world. Time and space pose no problem for the mind. Within it we can travel to China at the suggestion of the word or shrink to the size of an atom to explore

116

microscopic worlds. It can allow us to become anything the mind can conceive of.

One obvious advantage of using fantasy is that it can take you places you can't reach any other way. You can't take a field trip inside a petunia, but a guided fantasy can enable students to imagine themselves traveling through the plant and thus gives them a direct, personally meaningful experience that can transform a botany class into an exciting adventure. Fantasy can stimulate involvement and thus increase students' motivation to learn. It can offer students a new point of view and a new means of remembering information, and it can produce a "gut level" understanding that goes much deeper and will be remembered longer than the verbal presentation of a text or lecture. As the grammar unit mentioned in Chapter 1 demonstrates, fantasy has the power to help some students assimilate and use information which remains inaccessible when presented in more left-hemisphere modes.

While fantasy is a valuable teaching tool, it is also a thinking skill that every student should be taught to use. Beyond being a pleasant and motivating experience, the ability to transcend physical limitations through the mind, to project oneself into something and explore it mentally or to imagine oneself becoming the thing, is an extremely important skill for problem solving and other creative endeavors. One of the more dramatic examples of the power of this type of thinking, Albert Einstein's fantasy of himself riding a ray of light, played an important role in the discovery of the theory of relativity. Any lesson that employs fantasy addresses at least two instructional objectives—the mastery of subject matter and the mastery of an important thinking skill.

The power of fantasy is that it offers the fruits of right-hemisphere thinking and thus provides us with the resources of both sides of the brain. If you ask students to think about a noun, they will respond with information from the left hemisphere. If you ask them to become a noun and tell you how it feels, they will call up the insights of the right hemisphere.

Because fantasy is a right-hemisphere function, the process of fantasizing *feels* quite different from left-hemisphere processes.

Left-hemisphere cognition is active; the mind consciously manipulates ideas. Right-hemisphere thinking occurs without verbal awareness and therefore we are less conscious of it. In fantasy, we *receive* images from the right hemisphere; the process is a bit like watching a movie. Of course, in a movie the viewer has no control over the images while in fantasy a person can manipulate and direct the experience. The degree of control one exercises and how it is done is important. One cannot force a fantasy; trying too hard will block the flow of images. One can, however, create the conditions which allow images from the left hemisphere to reach consciousness easily.

The mind must be in a state of relaxed attention, alert and receptive to inner imagery. This receptive state is the key to fantasy. A suggestion is given ("You're inside a flower." "Become a seed."), and the mind waits for an image or series of images to arise. The images may be perceived visually or through other senses, or they may be translated to a word or phrase so quickly that we receive them as a verbal message. But while the imagery and the way we experience it vary with the individual, the receptive state is constant. You do not think about a flower or a noun—you imagine yourself experiencing or becoming the thing.

The point of view you assume during a fantasy has a major impact on the experience. You can imagine yourself as an observer, or you can identify with the subject of the fantasy and become that thing itself. In one case you imagine yourself inside a human heart; in the other you become the heart. Becoming the thing you're studying is a bit more challenging than observing it, but the identification stimulates deeper, more personal involvement. While both forms of fantasy generate inner sensory imagery, identification produces the added dimensions of kinesthetic experience and emotional response. Instead of watching the heart function, students feel the heart's contractions in their muscles and imagine how it would feel to move the blood through themselves. They may even experience emotions, such as pride at their importance or resentment of the never-ending work. In making a connection between the subject of the fantasy and their own bodies, students are using metaphorical as well as sensory thinking.[1]

The degree of involvement students experience during a fantasy is largely a function of how the teacher presents it. For some purposes you may want to slip fantasy into a regular lesson with very little change in pace. For others, you may want students to relax and go into a somewhat deeper fantasy state in which you guide some of their imagery. In the former case, you need make no special arrangements, but you should know exactly what you plan to say to elicit the fantasy experience. After describing how a thermometer works, you can ask students to become a molecule of mercury in a thermometer lying on a counter, then to imagine that the thermometer is being placed in a hot liquid and to describe what's happening to them there. For a slightly different lesson which would help develop hypothesis formation skills, you could give students the information that heat makes molecules more energetic but not tell them anything specific about thermometers, then ask them to become the molecule of mercury and to be aware of what happens to them when the thermometer is placed in the hot liquid.[2] A fantasy like this takes only a few minutes of time and gives many students a far deeper understanding of the subject.

EXPERIENCING FANTASY

Since the use of fantasy in the classroom has been relatively rare, few teachers have first-hand experience with it as a teaching technique. Fortunately, it is not difficult to learn, and you can teach yourself. The next section is designed to help you do just that. It includes two fantasies, one from the point of view of an observer and one that directs you to become something else. You can do the two fantasies one after the other or at separate times, but if you do them at different times, be sure to take time to relax and quiet your mind before each fantasy. If you've done quite a bit of both types of fantasy work, you may find that the directions provide a useful review and you may not feel the need to go through the fantasies yourself. However, if you have not experienced one or both types of fantasy, it is essential that you use the exercises to give yourself that experience before you use fantasy in your classroom. Fantasy is a case where reading cannot substitute for experience.

Preparations

1. Select a place that's comfortable and quiet. Any sounds, even quiet ones, will often turn up as part of your fantasy, and loud sounds will destroy your concentration. Most people find it easiest to do the relaxation and fantasy exercises while lying down on a couch or rug, but they can also be done while sitting in a chair. If the room is bright, you may want to darken it.

2. Select a time when you aren't rushed or preoccupied with other demands. Allow yourself twenty to thirty minutes so you can relax and enjoy the experience.

3. Ask someone to guide you through the fantasy. The guide does more than simply read the fantasy. He must pace his reading so that you move along smoothly, being careful not to rush, but also not waiting so long that you lose momentum. His voice should be pleasing; it should be clear without intruding on your fantasy. Give him the directions for guiding a fantasy on page 137. If you cannot find someone to serve as guide, you can act as your own guide by taping the fantasy on a tape recorder. Be sure to include the relaxation instructions.

4. Choose a living plant from your house or garden to study before the first exercise. It should be one you like, one whose textures and colors are pleasing to you. Just before the fantasy, take a few minutes to explore the plant. Look carefully at its different parts and their textures; see if it has a smell. You may even want to use a magnifying glass to see more clearly.

5. Most people concentrate better on fantasy with their eyes closed, but there are some individuals who prefer to leave their eyes open. If you don't close your eyes, let them relax and become passive, staring into space and not looking at anything in particular.

6. Finally, try to leave behind your preconceived notions of what fantasy should be like. The actual experience is different for each person. Some people see vivid imagery while others do not see as much as sense their imagery. Be receptive and attentive to the imagery in whatever form it takes, and it will become stronger and clearer with experience. If at any point you become uncomfortable with what's happening in your fantasy, you can change it or you can leave the fantasy by concentrating on your breathing and opening your eyes.

Relaxation and Fantasy. The first step in fantasy is to achieve a state of relaxed attention—that is, to shut off the verbalization of the left hemisphere so that the right can begin to be heard. For those who are highly verbal, shifting gears can be a bit difficult at first. The internal "voice" is so familiar that it's easy to identify it as oneself. Actually, it is only one of the many mental states we all have and, with practice, it can be switched on or off at will. Anytime you enter fantasy or use the technique with your class it is important to take a few moments to relax and shift gears. The exercise that follows is one way to do that for yourself. The dots indicate places where the guide should pause for several seconds.

EXERCISE 1 (*Relaxation Exercise*)

First get your body in a comfortable position, one in which you can relax easily. . . . Now close your eyes. . . . Become aware of your breathing. . . . Don't do anything about it, just be aware of how the air moves in and out. . . . Allow the air to move deep into your abdomen but don't force it. . . . Become aware of your feet. . . . Allow them to relax and feel warm and heavy. . . . Let that relaxed, warm heaviness spread up your legs . . . through your knees . . . your thighs . . . and into your body. . . . Imagine the relaxation spreading through your body . . . filling your stomach . . . chest . . . back . . . shoulders. . . . Let your arms relax . . . your hands. . . . Now feel your neck relaxing, becoming soft and warm. . . . Finally, let your face relax. . . . Let your jaw become loose and easy. . . . Feel your lips relax . . . your cheeks . . . your eyes . . . your forehead . . . and your scalp. . . . Continue to be aware of your breathing and take a moment or two to enjoy the way your body feels before we begin our fantasy journey.

EXERCISE 2 (*Observer Fantasy*)

Imagine that you are shrinking. . . . Allow yourself to become ever smaller until you are so tiny that you can fit into a drop of water. . . . Now, safe and comfortable within your water drop, you are slipping down into the ground through the soil. You come to rest on a tiny hair on the root of a plant. Take a moment to experience the moist soil and the roots around you. Feel the temperature. . . . Look around. . . . Listen for sounds. . . . Be aware of smells. . . . Discover that you can reach out of your drop and feel any surface you wish. You can leave your drop of water at any time if you feel like it. . . . Now you are being drawn into the plant through the tiny root hair. You are inside the root and you are being carried along inside the root as moisture and nourishment travel from there to the rest of the plant. . . . Experience the root. . . . Notice the sights . . . sounds . . . smells . . . how it feels . . . temperature. . . . We're moving into the stem now . . . being carried upward toward the leaves. . . . Look around you. . . . Notice how the stem is different from the roots. . . . Now you're moving into a leaf. What's happening around you? . . . Is the sun shining? . . . How does it affect the leaf? . . . Look around for colors and textures. . . . Be aware of sounds . . . and smells. . . . When you've finished exploring inside the leaf, slip out onto the surface. . . . Once you're out, look around. . . . Be aware of the difference between inside and outside. . . . Discover the textures . . . smells . . . and sounds. . . . If you feel like it, play on the surface—go for a hike . . . explore. . . . When you've spent as long as you'd like, you can hop off and float gently to the ground. You are so tiny that you will float softly and land gently. . . . Take a last look up at the plant you've traveled through and when you're finished, feel yourself returning to your normal size. . . . When you're ready you can return to the room and open your eyes. *Note to the guide: If you're going to do Exercise 3 at this time, omit the last line and say instead, "Allow your mind to stay relaxed and clear for a few moments before we go on to the next fantasy."*

EXERCISE 3 *(Identification Fantasy)*

Imagine that you are a seed. . . . Feel your round seed-body sleeping in the dry soil. . . . Now the rains start and the soil around you becomes wet. . . . Feel yourself drink in the moisture. . . . You are beginning to grow. . . . Feel your body growing inside your seed shell. . . . You are developing a root. . . . Feel it grow and press against your shell-skin. . . . The skin splits, feel your root push out into the dark, moist soil. . . . You're still growing. . . . Now your tightly curled seed leaves push upward. . . . Feel your seed body stretch out as your root grows out through the soil and your seed leaves push upward. . . . Look around you. . . . Listen to the sounds. . . . Smell the odors. . . . Feel the earth around you. . . . The tip of your seed leaves is just below the surface of the soil. . . . Feel yourself break

through. . . . Look around you at this new world. . . . Listen to its
sounds. . . . Feel the sun and air. . . . Smell the new smells. . . .
Feel yourself stretch up toward the sun. . . . Let your seed leaves
open. . . . And when you feel ready, bring your mind back to this
room and open your eyes.

After your fantasy experiences, take some time to review and
understand them. You can learn more about your own thinking
by being aware of which parts of the exercises were most easy and
most difficult for you. Smells come easily to some people, but are
difficult for others. Was your fantasy in color? Were you aware of
or did you actually hear sounds? Also be aware of the emotions
you experienced before, during, and after the fantasy. Many
teachers find that it helps establish trust and student involvement if they share their own experiences in class discussion. Students will feel much more like talking about their inner experience if you are also open about your feelings. Of course, it's
important that your experience does not seem to represent the
"right" way to do the exercise; share your difficulties as well as
your strengths.

The plant fantasy can be used with a wide range of ages and
subjects. For teachers just beginning to experiment with fantasy
lessons, it can serve as a possible first fantasy to use with your
class. If it's not applicable to your class, the idea of journeying
inside something can be adapted to any subject. In geometry, you
can explore various geometric figures from both inside and outside. In history the journey can take you back in time. In geography, you can explore a distant landscape, and for English, you can
step into a story or novel you're reading. In adapting the plant
fantasy, remember that a plant is fairly familiar to most people.
The source of your journey should also be familiar. The more your
students know about the subject of the fantasy the easier it will
be for them.

The seed fantasy can also be used in a variety of situations,
and the idea of becoming something in order to understand it
better can be applied to any subject.

The two exercises are designed to give you experience with
two types of fantasy. They are not, however, the only ways fan-

tasy can be done. As in the example of the thermometer presented earlier, you can do a short, powerful identification fantasy without a relaxation exercise and integrate it quite naturally into your teaching. Using fantasy this way is less threatening to both teachers and students because it doesn't feel like such a departure from familiar classroom activities. It has the advantage of requiring less classroom time, and it gives students valuable practice in making a quick, easy switch from analysis to identification and back again. You can experience this use of fantasy by selecting one of the exercises presented later in this chapter and simply doing it without any specific preparations. Become the thing it asks you to be and do the exercise aloud.

OBSERVATION FANTASIES

Introducing Material.   Fantasies like the plant journey are a fine way to introduce new material to a class. Used before students have read anything about the subject, they can create experience which makes the textbook presentation both easier to understand and more meaningful. In designing such a fantasy, it's best to avoid labels and technical terms. Instead, provide a brief description and leave the rest to students' imaginations. Labels often block perception because once we have a name for something, we tend to assume we understand it and don't feel a need to explore it further.

Be sure to at least outline your fantasy before you use it. An outline will insure you don't leave something out, help you anticipate and overcome difficulties in advance, and enable you to plan your descriptions for both accuracy and vividness. The plant journey would be fine as it is for younger students; if you used it for senior high school science, you'd probably want to go into greater detail about the inner structures of the plant which the students would be studying.

Reviewing.   Fantasy can also serve as a review technique, a means of helping students retain information. By generating sensory images which are connected to the material students want to retain, fantasy gives them a way to remember based on imagery as well as words. This approach is especially helpful for those who are less verbally oriented. Fantasies used for review differ from other types in several ways. First, the language is specific and includes labels and terms. Instead of directing them to "see how the water moves up the stem," you'll tell them to find the xylem, the tracheids, and the vessels and watch how each works. Be very explicit about the purpose of the fantasy. Tell students before you do it that it is a way of helping them remember and retain information for the exam. At the time of the exam remind them that the experiences and images from their fantasies can help them remember information for the test and encourage them to use these images.

A second way to use fantasy to review material is to give students a writing assignment which requires them to use fantasy. The following examples are from a tenth-grade biology class of Janet Patterson, Mt. Greylock Regional High School in Massachusetts.

This girl takes us on a metaphorical journey, describing the plant as an "applantment" house. Hattie walked up the tracheid stairway which had originally had substances in it; when the stairway was finished all the material had been removed, leaving only the hollowish stairwell. The builders had done this to make it easier for the water drops, who worked in the building to get up to the applantments. . . . (later in the leaf) The rooms on the bottom floor were rather haphazardly arranged, someone had once said they had as much organization as the holes in a sponge, so they called the first story the spongy layer. On the second story the rooms were all small, but with high ceilings. In this way the architect got a great number of rooms in contact with the sun.[3]

This boy is journeying into a plant in a tiny rocket boat and reporting back to Dr. Spoof. "You must be in the cortex by now," said Dr. Spoof. "What does it look like?"

"It's hard to explain, but it appears to me to be a lot of slimy brown tanks, all lined up in rows, each of them seems to be sort of translucent, as the light penetrates them."

Then up ahead their [sic] loomed another kind of wall, it was sort of white. I had hardly had a chance to look at it

when I was through it, when all of a sudden I saw a wall that
was red ahead.

"That must have been the endodermis and the pericy-
cle you just went through," the radio cackled after I told it
what I had seen.[4]

In preparing the assignment, be sure to specify what aspects of
the subject should be included. When assigning a journey through
a car engine, for example, provide a list of which mechanisms
should be described. A fantasy writing assignment not only stimulates creativity and improves writing skills; it also forces students to examine the subject in a new way and improves their
understanding of it. An additional advantage for teachers is that
it's more interesting to read than a straight review of facts. While
it's good to express appreciation of particularly creative or well-
written pieces, the criteria for grading should be thoroughness
and accuracy (see "Evaluating the Products of Fantasy" later in
this chapter for further suggestions).

IDENTIFICATION FANTASIES

Designing a Fantasy. Identification fantasies stimulate even
greater involvement than those in which students are observers.
Such fantasies require them to project themselves into the thing
they are imagining, to feel as it would feel. Some students find
them a bit more difficult than observer fantasies, but if the fantasies are designed properly, this problem can be eliminated.
Such a fantasy requires a script to draw the students into the
identification. The script tells them what they are to be and sets
the scene. Then it creates a dramatic situation in which the student becomes an actor. The script focuses student attention on the
aspect of the subject you've chosen for study.[5]

In the beginning you can help students get into fantasy
easily by choosing as your subject something with many human
attributes. Animals, especially those with which students are familiar and which they like, are easiest. A cat is easier than a
sloth both because students are more familiar with cats and be-

cause they're apt to like cats better. A skunk may be hard for some students at first because they don't want to identify with something that has negative associations for them. A lizard is easier than a snake because lizards have arms and legs, and snakes do not. Living things are easier than nonliving things; and, finally, machines that move are easier than those which do not. A refrigerator is harder than a washing machine because it sits passively while the washer spins and churns and gurgles through its washing cycle.[6]

Fantasy need not be limited to animals and machines. Students can become a nerve cell, a plague, a city, a document, or a dangling participle. In all cases, it is easier to become involved in a fantasy that includes physical action than one which does not. It's easier to identify with the Declaration of Independence during the Revolution when it could have become a death warrant for its signers than now when it's displayed in a glass case. The emphasis on making fantasy easy should not obscure the fact that more challenging fantasies can be very effective with a class that's had some experience with fantasy. One does not learn more by being the Declaration of Independence in 1776 than in the present. The two fantasies produce different insights, and the decision to use one instead of the other should be based on the teacher's goals and the students' experience.

The power of identification fantasies to stimulate deep involvement stems in part from their potential for emotional identification as well as from their sensory imagery. The emotions are an important part of the experience because they show that students are really identifying with the subject. The directions for the fantasy determine how great a role emotions are to play in it.

Muscular or kinesthetic identification takes students even deeper into the subject than emotional identification. When students can tell how their seed muscles feel, they are experiencing the fantasy fully. They have succeeded in making a connection between their bodies and the seed so that they're learning from inner experience. Kinesthetic imagery is also a means of achieving a "gut level" or working understanding which produces new insights.

In discussing an identification fantasy it's important to always use the first person. You cannot identify with the seed when you are thinking about how "it" would feel. Encouraging students to experience emotions and muscular imagery also helps strengthen the identification.

Identification fantasies can be used for the same purposes as observer fantasies—that is, to introduce new material, to review, and to stimulate writing. In addition, they can also be used at any point in a unit to help students understand and assimilate concepts. The thermometer fantasy suggested earlier is an example of this use of fantasy.

In designing a fantasy to help students assimilate a concept, it is crucial to choose the appropriate subject for them to identify with. The script should also include enough information to remind them of the most important facts about the subject. The following exercise from Gordon and Poze's *Teaching Is Listening* is an excellent example of this type of fantasy.

EXERCISE 4

You are the piston of an internal combustion engine. You do all the work. You suck in the air and gasoline mixture. You compress it so that it will burn with more power. You're the one that's exploded down when the mixture ignites. You turn the crankshaft and you do the cleaning up. You force out the burnt gases so that everything is ready for the next cycle. Describe what your "piston body" experiences as you go through the four cycles of internal combustion.[7]

In asking students to identify with the piston, the fantasy focused on the one mechanism which would allow them to experience all four steps of internal combustion. The choice of any other mechanism would have produced a more limited and less effective fantasy. The fantasy also included just the right amount of information to remind students of the four steps.

Choosing the Subject of a Fantasy. In all identification fantasies, the subject of the fantasy—the thing the students are asked to become—has a major impact on the focus of the unit, so it should be chosen carefully. As an example, let's take a history class studying the American colonial period and assume that the teacher's goal is to help students appreciate the difficulties faced by the colonists as they moved westward. After giving them some information on the subject she decides to use a fantasy. The obvious source of identification is the settler, but it may not be the best choice. Fantasies in which students identify with other people are fairly close to role-playing, and while they may create involvement, they may also produce stereotyped responses in which little new is learned. This problem can be avoided by asking students to become an object closely associated with the individual or group being studied; instead of becoming the settler, become the settler's cabin or the land being settled. The fantasies which follow will give you a chance to experience the difference between identifying with a person and with something else.

EXERCISE 5

You're a colonist in the Massachusetts Bay Colony. You and your family have moved from the relative safety of the larger settlements to a new town. Along with a few other settlers you've cleared land, and each of you has built a small sturdy wood cabin. It's September, and already the weather's turning colder; you're rushing to finish your preparations for winter before the snows come and leave you isolated in your little cabin. Become the colonist. How do you feel about your new home and the coming winter?

EXERCISE 6

You are the settler's cabin. You stand alone in a clearing, quite a distance from the nearest other house and many miles from the nearest settlement where food and supplies can be bought. You are small, yet you must shelter the settler's family and their supplies through the long winter. Become the cabin. Feel the first chilly blasts of wind. How do you feel?

EXERCISE 7

You are a piece of land in the Connecticut River Valley. For centuries you have been covered by deep forests, full of all sorts of birds and animals. From time to time an Indian tribe camps on you for a season and then moves on, and by the next year the signs of their presence are almost gone. But now, new men have come, men with axes to cut your trees and plows to dig your soil. One of these men has cleared a space and built a house from the trees he chopped down. You can feel the winter coming; your plants are preparing for the long, cold season. You watch the man prepare, too, hurrying to finish his little cabin and store his supplies. Become the land. How do you feel about this man and his cabin? . . . How do you feel about his plow? . . . How does your land-body experience the changes the men have brought?

While there may not seem to be a great deal of difference between the first two fantasies, the second is much more likely to produce original responses and yield new insights. Asked to become the settler, students easily fall back on conventional ideas from movies or television; their responses are in a sense preconditioned. When you ask them to become the cabin, you force them into a new point of view and require them to think about the situation in a new way. The third fantasy allows them to consider the same situation from a broader perspective. By mentioning the Indians, it enables students to consider the different impact of each group on the land and the interaction of environment and technology. The choice of whether to use the second or third fantasy or both together would have to depend on the teacher's goals.

Focusing on an object rather than a person is particularly important in situations where the subject arouses such strong emotion that it may overwhelm students and interfere with their ability to think clearly. The human tragedy of slavery is such a subject. If your goal is to develop empathy and involvement, identifying with the slave may be the best choice. But if your students already feel strongly about the subject, you may elicit more insights into the issues of slavery if you ask them to become the slave's collar or the merchant ship turned slaver.[8]

The possibilities for an identification fantasy are almost

limitless. In the previous history example, you could design the fantasy around the meeting house if you wanted to focus on the role of religion in the community. You could ask students to become the Charter of the Massachusetts Bay Colony to better understand the relationship between England and the colonies. Or you could look to the colonists' tools if you wanted to explore the impact of technology on environment and vice versa. The English plow was a fine piece of equipment which worked beautifully in the soft earth of Britain but quickly became pitted and twisted by the rocky soil of New England. The plow can function as a metaphor for the colonists themselves; for just as the demands of the colonies required the development of an American plow, they functioned to transform Englishmen into Americans. A discussion of the similarities and differences between the English plow and the new settlers could provide an exciting followup to the plow fantasy.[9]

It cannot be emphasized enough that there are no right answers in fantasy. Each student's experience will be unique. In the history fantasy of the newly settled land, some students may feel compassion for the settler, others may feel blind hatred and anger at his intrusion. Some may be excited by the idea of growing crops; others may feel violated by the plow. The diversity of reactions can provide the basis for lively and stimulating class discussions. The difference of opinion should be treated as a means of appreciating the complexity and the many sides of a question rather than as debates to prove the correctness of one point of view. Any good identification fantasy will generate divergent points of view. In the preceding example, change is a violation of the old, causing discomfort and even pain; but it is also an opportunity for something new and exciting to emerge. Class discussions can be organized around these seeming contradictions to help students see both sides of the issue.

While there are no right answers, some students are able to generate much richer fantasies than others. Such fantasies are elaborate and complex, demonstrating thinking that is original and that probes the subject more deeply. As students share their fantasies in class, everyone benefits from these students' contributions. They both inspire and provide a model for other students, as the insights generated in these fantasies become available to everyone. One must resist the temptation to praise outstanding fantasies in front of the class; to do so introduces a form of evaluation that may inhibit rather than encourage other students.

The emphasis in this chapter has been on the teaching of substantive material, but identification fantasies can be useful in skill-oriented subjects as well. The fantasy which follows can be used in any class where students are using tools, equipment, or instruments—art, shop, physical education, instrumental music, sewing, and so on.

EXERCISE 8

Today we're going to take a new look at a tool that we use; and, hopefully, we'll learn something about how to use it more effectively. We usually think about this tool in terms of how it serves us. Today we're going to look at ourselves and how we work from the tool's point of view. I'm going to ask you to work with the tool as you usually do but to imagine that you are the tool. Become the tool, give your tool-self a voice, and tell about how you're being used. Are you being allowed to do the best possible job? . . . What could your person do that would help you do your job better? . . . Feel your tool muscles do your work . . . and tell your person how you want to use those muscles.[10]

FANTASY AS A BASIS
FOR SELF-EXPRESSION

Students frequently complain that they don't know what to write about or that writing is boring. Often what they are really saying is that they don't know how to gain access to their imaginations. For these students, fantasy can provide that access. With repeated experiences which encourage them to use their imaginations, they can not only improve the quality of their writing assignments but also develop skill and facility in the conscious use of their inner worlds. Imagination, like a physical muscle, becomes stronger and better coordinated the more it is used.

A fantasy to stimulate writing can be as simple or complicated as you wish. In general, you'll do much less guiding than when you're teaching subject matter. You'll want to allow as much room as possible for students to develop their own unique fantasies. It's important to stay away from any setting or situation that might frighten children. You don't know what monsters you might unleash on them if you guide them into a dark cave, and you don't want to leave them with unresolved fears.

The three fantasies that follow illustrate ways in which fantasy can be used to stimulate writing.

EXERCISE 9

Select a piece of music that evokes strong images for you. Play it for the class (after a relaxation exercise and suitable introduction) and ask them to let the music suggest images, moods, feelings, and sensations to them. Tell them to be receptive to whatever comes to them as the music plays. Afterward, ask them to talk or write about the experience in either prose or poetry. You can start with prose and select the strongest images to form the basis for poetry; or one or two strong images may serve as the basis for a longer prose piece. This fantasy can also be used as a stimulus for an art project. If you use it for both visual and verbal expression, you might devote some class time to discussing how the experiences differed (some students will prefer writing, others painting; it's a matter of personal style).

EXERCISE 10

To be done in conjunction with a story or novel the class is reading. Select an interaction between characters where strong feelings are evoked. The scene should be powerfully presented, but the characters' feelings should be left to the reader to infer. Ask students to close their eyes and to become one of the characters. Read the scene and ask them to feel what their character is feeling. Tell them not to label the emotions but to experience them fully—ask them to be aware of how their bodies feel, to see if they experience the emotion more strongly in one part of the body, to be aware of any visual images. Afterward have them describe what they experienced; the writing should be in the first person and the present tense.

EXERCISE 11

Tell students they're going to have an adventure. Have them create a place in their minds; explore it and in the exploration encounter an obstacle. Have them find a way to overcome the obstacle and find a chest which contains something valuable to them. Open the chest and enjoy the reward.

EVALUATING THE
PRODUCTS OF FANTASY

Right-hemisphere techniques work best in an environment where there is a high level of trust; students must know that they won't be ridiculed or criticized, or they will retreat to the safety of silence. This is especially true for fantasy. Using fantasy in school is a new experience for most students. It is also more personal and therefore more threatening. A student's fantasies are, after all, a part of him, and if other students are allowed to make negative comments, giggle, or smirk, or if the teacher evaluates his fantasy as unsatisfactory, that can be a crushing blow. In fact, the products of any new technique should not be evaluated until students have had a chance to use it a number of times. Evaluating too soon can lead some students to give up because they aren't doing as well as they'd like. We all need a period of time to try out new ideas and techniques and become comfortable with them without the pressure of external judgment. After all, would you try fantasy for the first time on the day your supervisor came to evaluate you?

The fact that you don't evaluate fantasies does not mean that you can't evaluate the writing based on a fantasy once students have had some experience with it. You must be clear that it is the writing and not the fantasy that's being evaluated. Make your criteria very clear and show that you're evaluating how vividly the image is expressed and not the image itself. Herbert Kohl, the author of *36 Children* and *Reading, How To,* has a wonderful solution to the problem of grading writing assignments. He suggests that you have students do a lot of writing.

You collect each assignment and keep it in a file, and periodically you give students their files and ask them to select the best two or three papers and submit them for a grade. In this way you grade them on their best work and relieve some of the tension attached to practicing new skills. You also give them a maximum amount of writing practice while spending a minimum amount of time grading.[11]

USING FANTASY
IN THE CLASSROOM

Fantasy becomes easier the more you use it; with experience both the ability to generate images and confidence in the process improve. Nevertheless, many teachers feel anxiety about introducing fantasy into their classes. They are excited by the possibilities it offers, yet apprehensive about their students' reactions. As with all new experiences, the first few times may be a bit strained. Some students may feel nervous and get giggly. Certain age groups will resist closing their eyes. Fantasy can be a powerful experience for many children; expect excitement from some and silence from others. Don't be surprised to hear them telling of the "crazy" thing you did in class, since some children feel embarrassed to express enthusiasm straightforwardly and will "put down" the new experience. Sometimes the students you expect to react most negatively will surprise you; they may find fantasy an experience in which they feel successful and thus become quite enthusiastic about it.

It is important to be sensitive to the effects of fantasy on children who may be emotionally unstable. If you have students whose stability seems questionable, it's wise to speak to a counselor or school psychologist to determine whether fantasy might have negative effects on them. In general, if you begin with fantasies that are nonthreatening and unlikely to evoke extremely strong emotions, you should be able to assess the impact on any student you're concerned about by observing the individual and chatting casually after class.

It's always important to consider the effects a fantasy is

likely to have on students. Fantasies involve very personal images; you don't know what response your words might evoke. A birth fantasy that may seem harmless to you could have a devastating effect on a girl who's had an abortion. Because of its power, fantasy should be used with sensitivity, and experiences should be structured so they are positive. You can avoid problems by not using negative images and emotionally charged subjects, and by being sensitive to students' reactions during and after the fantasy.

You can use the fantasies in this chapter as a model for designing your own lessons. The usual pattern for a fantasy lesson is (1) a brief explanation of the subject and purpose of the fantasy (what you're doing and why), (2) a relaxation exercise,[12] (3) the fantasy, and (4) class discussion or a writing assignment. Relaxation is a skill that is learned through practice. The first time you do it, it's best to use a longer exercise, like the one presented with the plant fantasies. As students become more experienced they will need less help in relaxing and quieting their minds, and you can use shorter exercises. Some students may initially have difficulty directing attention to the part of the body they are to relax. They may not be able to feel a foot unless it's being touched by something else. Reassure them that body awareness grows with practice, and encourage them to continue doing the exercises as best they can.

In designing a fantasy, you should first answer several questions for yourself.

1. What is the purpose of the fantasy? Is it to stimulate involvement, aid in assimilation and understanding of material, review, or stimulate writing?
2. What material do you want to cover? What will students learn from the fantasy?
3. What point of view will you use? Will it be an observer or identification fantasy?
4. If it's an identification fantasy, what do you want the students to identify with? If it's an observer fantasy, what specifically do you want them to observe?

Once you've answered these questions, you should write out your fantasy and select a relaxation exercise. Until you've become experienced at guiding fantasy, it's a good idea to try out your lessons on a friend, spouse, or colleague and actually guide someone through the fantasy. The feedback will help you discover and correct any points that aren't clear. If you don't feel comfortable working with someone, at least practice the pacing of the fantasy by reading it aloud. A tape recorder can be helpful with this.

Some teachers like to darken the room when they do a fantasy; it's not essential, but it may make concentration easier for some students, and it's another way of helping students shift gears. Before beginning a fantasy ask students to get comfortable in their seats. If your room has space where they can lie down and you feel comfortable about that, you can let them lie down. Suggest that they close their eyes, but do not require it. Explain that while most people concentrate better on fantasy with their eyes closed, there are some individuals who find it easier with their eyes open. If any students don't want to close their eyes, suggest that they stare into space, let their eyes be passive, and not look at anything in particular. For the first several times, remind students before beginning the fantasy that if at any point they don't like what's happening in their fantasy, they can change it or they can leave it by concentrating on their breathing and opening their eyes.

In guiding a fantasy you should be aware of several things:

1. Try to speak in a tone that is soft and soothing. Your speech should be clear, but it should not intrude on the fantasy. By adopting a tone that is slightly different from your everyday speech, you help students shift into a relaxed, receptive state. They will come to associate that tone with fantasy, and it will help them make the transition.
2. Try to pace your reading so that it is slow but not so slow that you lose momentum. Pause for about seven seconds each time you make a new suggestion so that students will have time for their imagery to form (the fantasies in this chapter use dots to indicate places to pause).
3. At the end of the fantasy give students several minutes to finish their fantasies and bring their attention back to the room. Your fantasies should always end with directions to return to the room and open their eyes when they're ready.

After the fantasy allow time for comments and questions. With short fantasies it's possible to let students tell what happened, but a long recounting of fantasies can dissipate the excitement and involvement you've created. It's often best to ask questions like "What did _____ look like?" "Did you hear any sounds in the _____?" "How did your muscles feel when you _____?" and elicit a number of short responses. If you're using the fantasy to stimulate writing, keep talk to a minimum and direct the students' energies into their written work.

FURTHER APPLICATIONS

Fantasy has many uses beyond the ones described in this chapter. We have concentrated on applications related to writing and to the mastery of subject matter; however, fantasy can also make valuable contributions to students' awareness and sensitivity and to their development as integrated, well-balanced individuals.[13] There are several uses of fantasy which fall between the cognitive and affective domains; while they do not deal with subject matter, they can greatly improve student performance. Many students are victims of negative imagination—that is, they imagine themselves failing. In stressful situations, they allow their minds to fill with worry and self-defeating images which make it impossible for them to succeed. Making students aware of the effect negative images have on them is a first step in confronting the problem.

Exercise 1 in Chapter 7 (page 160) can be used to give students experience with the effect that thoughts can have on performance and can stimulate discussion on ways in which people defeat themselves with negative images and failure messages. Awareness of self-defeating images is a first step in overcoming them. You can suggest to students that the next time they become aware of a fear or failure image they consciously change it and imagine instead that they are succeeding.[14]

Beverly Galyean, a Los Angeles consultant in confluent education, has demonstrated that guided fantasy can produce a more positive set toward learning. Working with low-achieving high school students (the lowest quartile on reading tests) in an inner city high school, she reports that five minutes of guided imagery at the beginning of class each day resulted in a decrease in disruptive behavior over a three-month period. Students became more attentive and responsive to the teacher and reported that they felt their grades and concentration had improved. The imagery was "designed to help the students focus on their inner strengths, view themselves as potentially successful and see the teacher as a helper in their quest for success. . . . The meditation activity seems to be a key factor in the kids' settling down, not only in the experimental class . . . [but] in other classes and at home."[15]

Some students have a great deal of difficulty in disciplining themselves to study and in concentrating on their work. Positive images can help them establish more effective habits. For this type of exercise to succeed, it must be repeated a number of times, but it's easy to do and requires only a few moments a day. To try it in your classroom, start ten days or so before a test or paper and take a few minutes at the beginning or end of class to do the following fantasy with your students.[16]

EXERCISE 12

Imagine yourself studying for the test (or paper). Decide where you'll study and take a few minutes to get a clear picture of the place. . . . Now put yourself in the place. . . . Get in a comfortable position and make sure you have what you need to study. . . . Now experience what it's like to concentrate on your work . . . to feel that you're understanding it . . . to know that you'll do well on the test (or paper).

You should explain that although fantasies do not substitute for study, they may make it easier for some students to relax and study more effectively. Before the test take a few minutes to let students relax and use the following fantasy.

EXERCISE 13

First I want you to empty your mind of all negative thoughts. Let go of any worries and any nervousness. . . . Allow yourself to feel calm and relaxed and alert. . . . The material you've studied is stored inside your mind; all you have to do is relax so that you can find it when you need it. Imagine yourself taking the test. . . . You're doing very well. . . . You're working calmly but quickly, even enjoying yourself because you know you're doing well. . . . See yourself finishing and handing in your paper. . . . Let yourself feel confident and proud of how well you've done. . . . Now keep the calmness and all those positive feelings with you as you open your eyes and begin the test.

This type of fantasy can be used in any situation where an individual wants to change behavior. If you want to experiment with it yourself, select a situation in your personal or professional life in which you would like to act differently than you usually do, such as getting up earlier or more easily in the morning, remaining calm despite provocation from certain students or colleagues, or speaking confidently before a group. Set aside a few moments during the day to relax, quiet your mind, and imagine yourself in the situation. Make the imagery as clear as possible; look carefully at your surroundings and feel yourself in the scene. Imagine yourself acting as you'd like to act—feeling alert or calm or confident. Really experience those feelings; make the fantasy as vivid as possible for yourself. In most cases if you repeat this fantasy every day for a week, you should experience some change in the way you act and feel in that situation.

CONCLUSION

From introducing a unit in biology to helping students develop better study habits, fantasy is indeed a versatile tool. One of the exciting side effects of teaching through fantasy is that it gives students a skill they can apply to many areas of their lives. In one high school English class, a girl came up to the teacher several days after a fantasy lesson and proudly described how after a quarrel at home she'd imagined herself being her mother, and the fantasy had helped her understand her mother's feelings. Then with a hint of a smile and a knowing look she said, "Then I fantasized that I was you. And now I understand . . ." What exactly she understood was never revealed, but she *did* pass a grammar test for the first time that quarter.

NOTES

1. As discussed in Chapter 4, metaphorical thinking involves making a connection between two seemingly unlike things. In this case the connection is between the student and the subject of the fantasy. In the model developed by Synectics Education Systems (SES), whose work on metaphor was discussed in Chapter 4, identification fantasies are referred to as personal analogies. See WILLIAM J. J. GORDON and TONY POZE, *Teaching Is Listening* (Cambridge, Mass.: Porpoise Books, 1972), pp. 70–89, for direction in writing lessons based on personal analogy.
2. For an example of a lesson using fantasy to teach about thermometers, see WILLIAM J. J. GORDON and TONY POZE, *Strange and Familiar, Book III* (Cambridge, Mass.: Porpoise Books, 1975), pp. 5–9.
3. ANDREA VERSENYI, a student at Mt. Greylock Regional High School, Williamstown, Mass., 1976.
4. Unidentified student at Mt. Greylock Regional High School, Williamstown, Mass., 1976.
5. GORDON and POZE, *Teaching Is Listening,* pp. 70–89.
6. Ibid., pp. 72–73.
7. Ibid., pp. 85–86.
8. Ibid., pp. 83–85.
9. The metaphor of the English plow was suggested by WILLIAM J. J. GORDON at a synectics workshop in Cambridge, Mass., 1975.
10. TONY POZE at Zephyros workshop, Venture Lodge, Pescadero, Calif., 1971.

11. This idea was referred to in HERBERT KOHL's column "Insight" in *Teacher* magazine.
12. For relaxation exercises, see GAY HENDRICKS and RUSSELL WILLS, *The Centering Book* (Englewood Cliffs, N.J.: Prentice-Hall, 1975) and GAY HENDRICKS and THOMAS B. ROBERTS, *The Second Centering Book* (Englewood Cliffs, N.J.: Prentice-Hall, 1977).
13. The "Transpersonal, Affective, and Confluent Education" section of the Bibliography will be helpful to teachers interested in expanding their activities in this area.
14. For exercises to combat negative thoughts and images, see R. H. McKIM, *Experiences in Visual Thinking* (Monterey, Calif.: Brooks/Cole, 1972), pp. 100–2.
15. *Brain-Mind Bulletin,* 5, No. 3 (December 17, 1979). For further information see BEVERLY GALYEAN, "The Effects of a Guided Imagery Activity on Various Behaviors of One Class of Low Achieving Students," Ken Zel Consultant Services, 767 Gladys Ave., Long Beach, CA 90804.
16. These two fantasies are based on techniques described in MAXWELL MALTZ, *Psycho-Cybernetics* (New York: Simon & Schuster, 1968). Maltz presents a method for changing behavior and replacing failure messages with images of success.

MULTISENSORY
LEARNING

In Western culture we tend to consider mind and body as separate entities, assigning thought to the mind and action and sensation to the body. However, the sensory and motor systems are part of both the brain and body, and their proper development is a prerequisite to successful cognitive functioning. The senses are the means by which we take in information; they tell us what we know about the world around us and form the basis for the development of abstract thought. In their early years, children use all their senses to learn about the world. They handle a new object, look at it from all sides, listen to any sound it makes, smell it, and often put it in their mouths both to taste it and to explore it with their tongues. By taking in information through all the senses they come to "know" the attributes of that object. Only later will they associate verbal labels with the object and its attributes.

The sensory system includes not only the five senses of sight, hearing, touch, smell, and taste through which we take in information about the world outside us, but also the proprioceptive senses—the kinesthetic, vestibular, and visceral systems which monitor internal sensations. The vestibular system, located in the inner ear, registers body position, movement, direction, and speed; it also plays an important role in interpreting visual stimuli. The kinesthetic system is located in the muscles, joints, and tendons and gives us information on body movement. The visceral system provides sensations from internal organs.

To understand the functioning of the sensory system, let's take a simplified look at what happens when a child handles a cube. As her fingers move over the cube's surface, sensory receptors in the skin of her fingers and hands (the tactile system) send messages to the brain with information about how the cube feels; at the same time receptors in her muscles and joints (the proprioceptive-kinesthetic system) send information on the movement of her fingers and hands. In the brain sensations from the touch and movement systems are integrated to give a "picture" of the object. If the child is looking at the cube, the visual system also supplies information to the brain, and signals from all three systems create an image of the object. Through this experience, the child builds up a concept of a cube and its attributes; she moves from sensory experience to concept formation.

The auditory, visual, and tactile-kinesthetic senses form the major learning modalities—that is, the primary pathways by which information is taken in. The learner is like a television set which can receive information on several channels. Usually, one channel comes in more clearly and more strongly than the others and the learner may come to rely on that channel as the primary means of learning and expression. In some cases a given channel may be plagued by "static interference," that is, for some reason information does not come in clearly. This situation creates the potential for a learning disorder.

Visual processing is so important that it has already been covered in a separate chapter. Auditory processing, while vitally important in learning, is largely beyond the scope of this book because it is primarily verbal. The aspect of auditory processing which does seem to be associated with the right hemisphere is music, and we will explore its applications to learning in this chapter. We will also discuss the roles of tactile and kinesthetic experience and perception as well as those of the senses of smell and taste. Since the role of multisensory learning is greatest in the early grades, we'll begin there.

SENSORY LEARNING IN THE EARLY PRIMARY GRADES

A child's brain is not just smaller or less experienced than an adult's; it is different in a number of ways. The brain develops all through childhood. Auditory perception and discrimination, tactile differentiation, and the ability to transfer information across sense modalities and to interpret that information are not complete until a child is at least eight years old. Development of visual perception continues into adolescence.[1] Therefore, in considering the role of the senses in learning, we must be concerned not only with how they can help children learn skills and information but also with how development affects a child's ability to perform specific tasks and with the impact of classroom activities on sensory development and integration.

Just as the brain develops in an orderly manner, thinking progresses in a predictable sequence with verbal ability appearing relatively late in the process. A task must be appropriate to a child's level of development if the child is to succeed at it and grow from the experience. When we force children to learn to read and to work with verbal materials before they are developmentally ready, we are like a builder who, eager to see results, fails to put in the foundation before beginning work on the house.

The sensory and motor systems form the foundations for later development of both verbal and abstract thought. Skills like reading and writing require complex coordination of these systems. Children who have not achieved sufficient sensory-motor integration will experience learning difficulties. For many, time will solve the problem; their neural systems will mature and the children will be ready to read. If children are in a class where reading is emphasized before they're developmentally able to do it, they experience themselves as "stupid" and develop negative attitudes toward school and their own competence. By the time their neural systems are ready for reading, psychological barriers may prevent many of them from learning.

Even children who have no such problems are often asked to perform tasks inappropriate to their developmental level and thus do not use their minds in the most productive manner. With our emphasis on verbal processes, we forget that much high-level thinking is not verbal. When you did the exercises in Chapter 3, you used nonverbal strategies to solve problems you couldn't solve verbally. When children build a birdhouse or play a strategy game (any game that involves more than luck), they are using high-level nonverbal thinking—planning, visualizing, predicting—which will serve them well in school and beyond. Ditto sheets and workbooks develop a limited set of thinking skills and are often much less intellectually challenging than many games.

Let's look at the impact of an emphasis on reading and a heavy reliance on printed materials on a hypothetical classroom of first graders. Some students will be unable to work successfully because they are developmentally immature; their brains and bodies simply aren't ready to do the assigned tasks. They need more time and more sensory and motor experience, but instead of getting that experience, they are sitting at desks struggling with tasks which produce anxiety, frustration, and feelings of failure that may persist through their entire school experience. A few students may suffer from poor sensory-motor integration; they will not "grow out of it." Without the help of a learning disabilities specialist, they will fail and continue to fail.

The majority of students will probably be able to perform the work assigned with varying degrees of success. A few will do so easily; most will work hard and receive their gratification from external praise, never experiencing the internal reward of discovering meaning for themselves. They will be coping, learning by rote because they are not yet developmentally capable of fully understanding the material they're encountering. As an example, learning that $3 + 2 = 5$ is very different from discovering that three of any kind of thing can be added to two of anything, and it will always make five things. The first is a set of symbols which can be memorized; the second is an understanding of a mathematical concept which can be used to develop further understanding of mathematical relations. To teach children too early so that they learn by rote is to deprive them of the joy and excitement of meaningful discoveries. It fills their heads with things they "know" but do not understand.

What is the alternative to this "paper and pencil classroom" with its heavy reliance on dittos and books? It is a classroom organized around experiences which stimulate *all* types of thinking—not just linear processes. Such a program recognizes that thinking develops as children are challenged to use their minds, that intelligence involves nonverbal as well as verbal processes, and that in young children nonverbal abilities are more highly developed than verbal ones (they can understand and do far more than they can express verbally). It would include perceptual-motor experiences—games which develop kinesthetic, tactile, auditory, visual, and graphic thinking;[2] a math program based on manipulation of real objects; an experientially based science program like SCIIS (Science Curriculum Improvement Study), which allows students direct experience with the phenomena and organisms being studied; a music program that combines music and movement to develop children's ability to repeat and compose simple melodies and rhythms; art activities using a variety of media; a wide selection of books and printed materials; a dramatic arts program; and games which stimulate logical thinking and problem solving. Hans G. Furth and Harry Wach designed such a program based on Piaget's theories; it is described along with directions for 179 of their thinking games in *Thinking Goes to School* (see "Kinesthetic and Multisensory Learning" in the Bibliography).

In such a classroom, the developmentally immature students have the time and experience they need and are spared the stigma of failure. The learning disabled students are easily recognized and can receive the help they require. And all children are able to enjoy a rich variety of experiences appropriate to their own developmental level through which nonverbal thinking can develop and mature. Children are able to build on their strengths but are also exposed to areas they might otherwise ignore and can thus develop new competencies. This type of learning is enjoyable and intrinsically rewarding. It does not establish the habit of learning by rote but instead develops high-level thinking and reasoning skills. It provides a solid foundation for later learning so that *all* children can experience success.

SENSORY-MOTOR INTEGRATION

The crucial roles of sensory perception and motor development are nowhere more clear than in the learning disabilities specialist's classroom, for here we see students whose difficulties in this area interfere with their ability to perform academic tasks. These are students of average or above-average intelligence who for a variety of reasons have special learning problems. Some can decode (read aloud) but do not comprehend what they're reading, some can read numbers but not letters, and many have multiple problems. Twenty years ago these students were dismissed as "dumb" (Albert Einstein, Thomas Edison, and Auguste Rodin all had such difficulty in school that their teachers viewed them as failures). Today we recognize that the performance of these students does not reflect their intelligence and that the problems which interfere with their learning can often be solved.

While there are a number of approaches to learning disabilities, a major area of focus is on the sensory-motor development of the child. The input of sensations and the output of motor activity must be integrated if a child is to function effectively. The muscles that control the eye must move smoothly, correctly, and without conscious control if a student is to visually scan a line of print; handwriting requires not only fine motor coordination of the arm, hand, and fingers, but balance of the entire body and integration of visual and auditory stimuli. Furth and Wach point out that:

> the importance of movement thinking should not be under-estimated. If the six-year-old child does not have fundamental control over both general and discriminative movements, he will find it difficult, if not impossible, to move his eyes across the page, look up and down from the chalkboard to his

> paper, hold a pencil, or compete in play with his peers. . . . If
> bodily movement is well under control, children can expend
> minimum energy on the physical mechanics of the task and
> maximum energy on the thinking related solution.[3]

Parents and teachers who notice that a child has poor motor coordination and is also having difficulty learning academic subjects should investigate the possibility of a learning disorder. Not all children who lack coordination are learning disabled, and not all learning disabled children have coordination problems, but there is a connection in enough cases to warrant screening students who show both deficits.[4]

The work in sensory-motor integration has important implications for all parents and teachers. Since sensory and motor development are aspects of neural processing and of the development of thinking and reasoning skills, young children should be given as many opportunities to move in as many ways as possible. Most children have an inner sense of the types of movement their body/mind needs. Just as they knew to stand and walk, they know to spin and balance. When young children spend hours spinning or standing on their heads or jumping, they are meeting some inner developmental need which we as adults should honor. With our crowded city streets, small apartments, and the seduction of television, many children do not get the variety of movement experiences they need; some specialists believe that this lack of movement contributes to the learning disorders we see in school. Given the importance of movement in a number of areas— physical development and well-being, self-image, and neural organization—movement education should be an important part of primary schooling. It is essential to go beyond dodgeball and relays to encourage the full range of motor development.

KINESTHETIC AND TACTILE LEARNING

The kinesthetic sense provides the third major mode for learning (auditory and visual are the other two). Kinesthetic and tactile learning are sometimes linked together though they actually involve different systems. The tactile system involves receptors in the skin. When you run your fingers over a surface, your tactile system gives you information on texture, shape, and temperature. The kinesthetic system registers movement; its receptors in the muscles and tendons provide information on body movement. When you are typing and you realize you've made an error even before you check the page, it's your kinesthetic system recognizing that the movement sequence was wrong. Your body/mind knows how a word should feel as well as look.

Too often in school we overlook the kinesthetic component of learning, since it is usually outside of conscious awareness. When you are unsure of the spelling of a word and write it down, you are relying on your kinesthetic sense to guide your hand (though you probably also rely on a visual check to see if the word looks right). When you use your hands to gesture as you explain something, you are using both kinesthetic and verbal thinking. Try consciously to keep your hands still as you talk; you're likely to find that it interferes with your efforts to clarify your ideas. Though we are generally unaware of it, gesture not only helps communication but also facilitates thinking and expression.

The kinesthetic-tactile senses are the third major channel for taking in information and remembering it. When we tell students to copy a spelling word ten times, we're using both kinesthetic and visual pathways. When we have them work with math manipulatives or build models, we're using both channels. For young children it is absolutely essential to provide this type of learning. Their inner "picture" of their world should be based on information from all the senses. For older children inclusion of kinesthetic experience has three advantages: It provides an additional way of understanding a subject, develops a valuable thinking modality, and gives kinesthetic learners a much better chance of success in the classroom.

While the majority of students prefer the auditory or visual channel, there are some who are primarily tactile-kinesthetic. These children are less able to learn by hearing and seeing than by touching and moving. For them information is taken in most easily through their hands and through movement. They like to handle things, to move them around, to move themselves around.

The concreteness of kinesthetic experience may help them if they have difficulty with abstraction. Unfortunately, we know less about kinesthetic learners than about those who are primarily auditory or visual. There are fewer kinesthetic learners, and often they have problems expressing themselves verbally. Learning disabilities specialists are usually a good resource in this area. They are generally more aware of strategies for helping kinesthetic learners because these children often end up in their classes. Specialists use tactile materials like sandpaper letters and substances of different textures and shapes. They also have students learn math facts or spelling words while bouncing on a rebounder or minitrampoline, clapping, or writing large letters and numbers in the air.

The value of kinesthetic experience is not limited to helping kinesthetic learners. Bob McKim describes the role of this type of thinking:

> Consider the sculptor who thinks in clay, the chemist who thinks by manipulating three-dimensional molecular models, or the designer who thinks by assembling and rearranging cardboard mockups. Each is thinking by seeing, touching, and moving materials, by externalizing his mental processes in a physical object.
>
> Externalized thinking has several advantages over internalized thought. First, direct sensory involvement with materials provides sensory nourishment—literally "food for thought." Second, thinking by manipulating an actual structure permits serendipity—the happy accident, the unexpected discovery. Third, thinking in the direct context of sight, touch, and motion engenders a sense of immediacy, actuality, and action. Finally, the externalized thought structure provides an object for critical contemplation as well as a visible form that can be shared with a colleague or even mutually formulated.[5]

KINESTHETIC LEARNING
IN ACADEMIC SUBJECTS

Math Manipulatives.   In math, materials that rely on manipulation of objects have the double advantage of offering concrete experience as the basis for understanding concepts and providing kinesthetic stimulation so that children receive information through two modalities. Patricia Davidson, whose work on math styles was discussed in Chapter 2, points out that it's important to distinguish between materials that use a discrete or set approach and those that use a continuous or length approach, and that both should be included in a program. A discrete (set) approach uses counters and grouping of objects—for example, a single popsicle stick equals one, ten sticks in a cup equals ten, ten cups of ten sticks each on a plate equals one hundred. A continuous (length) approach relies on measurement and spatial sense—for example, ten unit blocks placed in a row are the same length as the single ten rod. This type of activity relies more on spatial perception than on counting.[6]

Mary Baratta-Lorton's *Math Their Way* offers a program of activities using concrete materials primarily in a discrete approach. Its sequenced activities use familiar, easily available materials to teach such basic cognitive skills as logical thinking and pattern recognition while also introducing and elaborating basic mathematical concepts and operations. Cuisinaire rods and powers of ten blocks use a continuous approach in which students can see relationships represented spatially. Both types of materials should be an important part of any elementary math program, and all students should be encouraged to use them. While both present the same concepts, some students will learn more quickly from one type of material than the other, and each type contributes to the development of different but equally important mental functions.

Finger math offers another means of teaching math through tactile, kinesthetic, and visual channels, though it is certainly no substitute for manipulatives. It should not be confused with the type of counting on fingers that young children do; it is a far more sophisticated system. Based on the Japanese abacus, finger math has students use their fingers to add, subtract, multiply, and divide. Teachers report that this approach helps slow learners master computation and challenges gifted students to discover new applications, thus motivating and involving students of all ability levels. However, students who have problems with fine motor coordination have difficulty with finger math.

Movement Games. Movement games that teach concepts not only provide kinesthetic stimulation for learners; they also help release the physical energy that makes it difficult for children to attend to stationary activities. Sheila Kogan of the Richmond Public Schools, Richmond, California, creates movement games to teach math and language skills. In one game she begins with a pile of five foam blocks and asks each student to estimate how many he can jump over; the student must then tell her how many blocks must be added or taken away to get the desired number. To develop vocabulary she plays a game in which she calls out a command like "on top of" or "next to," and has students scramble to put themselves in an appropriate place. Once a teacher has established an orderly way of introducing movement into the classroom (see Kogan, *Step by Step,* in the Bibliography for techniques for accomplishing this), movement games can be used to teach a variety of concepts, to develop problem-solving strategies, and to practice motor skills.

Dance. Dance can also contribute to academic learning and to the development of creativity, especially when students are encouraged to make up their own movement patterns. Joyce Boorman's *Dance and Language Experiences with Children* provides excellent activities that show children how to experience "tasting words with their bodies, with their minds, with their tongues."[7] She gives words meaning through movement. Students are encouraged to explore words like *threading, gliding, swirling,* and *lingering* through movement. Boorman describes the process as "painting word pictures in space." The natural extension of the movement experience is the use of the words in creating poems. The following poem was written by a third grader after one of Boorman's dance experiences:[8]

> *I'm the wind*
> *Swirling, whirling up I go*
> *Up down, all around.*
> *I twist and turn all for fun*
> *I whip and drip*
> *I blow and roll*
> *I'm the wind.*

I find the kind of place I like
I take your hat away from you
and put it on my head.
I'm the wind for sure.
ALEIDA LAUCIRICA (GRADE 3)

The movement thus provides the basis for building vocabulary, stimulating creativity in both the kinesthetic and verbal modes, improving writing skills, and contributing to motor development. In addition, the linking of movement and writing may help kinesthetic students who sometimes have trouble with verbal expression. It also creates a powerful experience which gives students something that is personally meaningful to communicate and is thus much more likely to stimulate good writing. The Orff-Schulwerk System, which will be discussed in the section on music later in this chapter, also uses movement and sound improvisation.

Chapter 8 will discuss many techniques which could be classified as kinesthetic-tactile or multisensory. Any time one teaches from direct experience, students are able to approach the subject in the way that best suits them; the kinesthetic-tactile students are able to handle and manipulate real objects or to move around as part of a simulation. Such opportunities are especially important for them.

Gesture.   Gesture is the kinesthetic component of communication; it can also aid memory. Students in general and particularly those who are primarily kinesthetic can improve their memories by putting a gesture to each thing they need to remember. Once the word and gesture are associated in their minds, they can often retrieve the word by using the gesture. In fact, the Total Communication approach to teaching children with language and communications disorders uses signing and talking simultaneously. Its proponents believe that gestures help cue verbal memory. For some students, the teacher's use of hand gestures as she talks probably helps them to both pay attention and "get the feel" of the subject.

In Suggestology (see page 165) foreign language classes,

teachers put gestures to the phrases they teach. Each time teachers use a phrase, they make the associated gesture, and students are encouraged to do the same. Just as humming a tune can help one recall the words of a song, making a gesture can help students remember a phrase. In addition, gestures are an important part of communication in many countries, and students communicate much better if they have a gestural as well as a verbal vocabulary.

Movement and Thinking.   An additional aspect of kinesthetic learning worth noting is the role that movement plays in some individuals' thinking. For some people it is extremely difficult to think while sitting still. They need to pace or move in some other way. As adults we often have this freedom; yet it is rarely extended to students. Obviously, one cannot have a classroom full of pacing students, but just as it's important to provide a quiet corner for students easily distracted by visual or auditory stimuli, so it is important to make some provision for students who work better if they're allowed to move. Chewing gum and pencil tapping are sometimes signs that students are trying to find an outlet for their movement needs. While these actions may be extremely annoying to teachers, for some students they are an effort to cope with demands that are at variance with their own bodies' needs. With the student whose energy level is such that sitting still for a period of time is difficult, it is unrealistic to expect total immobility. Instead the teacher and student should try to find a form and level of movement that both can live with ("Tap your fingers on your leg, not on the desk," or "Chew gum but don't pop it.").

KINESTHETIC PERCEPTION
IN PHYSICAL LEARNING

The areas of education most clearly associated with kinesthetic perception and learning are those which involve training the body, including not only physical education but such subjects as typing, sewing, music (instrumental), and shop. These are the subjects in which students have the opportunity to learn not only specific movement patterns but also how to use kinesthetic feedback to improve motor skills. Just as a science teacher's job is to teach both the concepts of science and the thinking processes required to function in that discipline, teaching that involves physical performance should cover both the specific movement sequences and the process of kinesthetic awareness that underlies all movement. Too often students are shown how to do something and told to do it. For a student who already possesses good kinesthetic abilities, such instruction may be enough; for many other students it is not. They experience themselves as incompetent and struggle to develop coping strategies which will enable them to perform the activity but which often involve using their bodies in ways that are only minimally effective.

Kinesthetic awareness is an inner sense, an awareness of how the body feels as it moves, how muscles feel when they are tense or relaxed. Students often function automatically with little awareness of what they're doing. They do not realize that their jaws or shoulders are overly tense or that their heads are filled with chatter that distracts their attention. Teaching about kinesthetic awareness must focus attention inward to bodily sensations rather than words. Most students have very little experience with this concentrated, nonverbal attention to muscle sensations, but becoming aware of it and practicing its use can improve their performance.

The importance of kinesthetic awareness was demonstrated in an experiment in 1952 by the late Lloyd Percival, director of Toronto's Sports College. Coleman R. Griffith, a psychologist, had observed that basketball players depended too much on sight when shooting and didn't make enough use of feedback from their muscles. Percival selected two groups of basketball players of matching ability, with an average score of twenty to twenty-one baskets in fifty attempts. The first group practiced predetermined shots for twenty minutes in the regular way. The second group practiced the same shots for the same amount of time, but they shot five minutes with their eyes open, ten minutes blindfolded while an observer told them exactly where each shot went and urged them to attend to muscle sensations, and then five minutes without blindfolds. After four weeks, the first group averaged twenty-three out of fifty baskets, while the second scored thirty-nine out of fifty.[9]

When students approach a new physical task, they have no way of knowing how it feels to move correctly; they must rely on the teacher to help them discover that. When the teacher offers only verbal directions, it's hard for students to develop kinesthetic awareness. Providing a visual model—that is, a chance to watch someone demonstrate the movement—is usually more helpful because it provides a mental image, and the body probably works from images rather than words. More helpful still is guiding the students' bodies with one's own so that they can feel the correct movement. The use of blindfolds described here can be applied to areas other than basketball, but the learner must have a means of accurate feedback. In wrestling or the martial arts, an opponent provides feedback; in other situations students can work in teams as they did in the Percival experiment.

There is a role for verbal instructions in kinesthetic learning. They can focus attention on how specific parts of the body should feel during an action as, for example, in an exercise class, "You should feel the stretch in your upper back," or "Your neck should be relaxed while you do this." They can also give students a visual or kinesthetic image to guide their movements; for example, in tumbling, "Become a ball, feel your 'ballness' as you roll, you're all curves and roundness" (notice that the statements are all phrased positively; telling students what not to do presents their minds with an image you don't want to put there). Phrases like "Feel your arm move like _____" "Become a _____," "Imagine that you're _____" are ways of suggesting images to guide movement. Images carry a sense of wholeness and integration; they also focus attention on a single point, which aids concentration.

On the other hand, verbal directions that concentrate on where to put the feet or what to do with the right arm may not give students a sense of how the movement is supposed to feel. The students may become so concerned with the parts that their movement becomes choppy and poorly coordinated. Smooth movement does not come from the head issuing verbal orders to the body, which is exactly how some verbal students operate. It comes from the body developing an inner sense of movement. In most, if not all cases, that inner sense comes most easily when one has a sense of the whole motor sequence. Once the whole is established, working on a specific part of it may be very helpful, but teaching the sequence as a set of discrete parts will confuse and misguide many students.

Sometimes students bring an old, incorrect motor program to the new task, as, for example, when a child who never learned to throw a ball correctly tries to play baseball or when one who has poor posture tries to learn to type. Then the teacher has a more difficult task, for established motor patterns do not change easily. Once a student has been standing or throwing incorrectly for a period of time, that way of moving feels natural, and change requires a good deal of experience with the new pattern as well as constant attention to eliminate the old one. It is important to realize that relapses to the old, incorrect pattern are not a sign of laziness; they are a sign that the body is still providing feedback that defines the old movement as correct, or that under stress it is reverting to the older pattern. The new pattern is not yet internalized; the student's body needs more practice with the correct one.

Part of kinesthetic awareness is learning to operate without undue stress. The ability to tense only the muscles needed to perform an action while relaxing those not in use enables individuals to move more effectively. It both reduces fatigue and eliminates blocks to necessary movement; for example, in typing, tension in the shoulders prevents the fingers from functioning at peak efficiency. Watch a group of students engaged in movement. Some will move easily, while others will reveal a constricting tightness in one or more parts of their bodies. Tension is most often the result of insecurity, a reaction to fear that one is not succeeding. It establishes a vicious cycle: Students who feel they can't type or shoot baskets become tense whenever they engage in that activity; their tension further exacerbates the problem, makes them less able to perform, and thus produces more anxiety and more tension.

In recent years there has been increasing interest among professional and Olympic athletes and coaches in training techniques that involve relaxation and imagery rehearsal. These techniques train the mind and body to work together to produce optimal performance. At present their application has been primarily outside the schools, but they offer a powerful resource for teachers in any area requiring physical skills. Their goals of building concentration, replacing anxiety with a positive mental set, and improving performance through multisensory imagery rehearsal (a form of fantasy) are as appropriate for education as for the sports arena.

A student's mental set affects both physical and academic achievement. Just as students who think they're poor in math are more likely to fail that subject, students who think they type slowly will fulfill that negative prophecy. The ability of the mind to limit the body's achievement is illustrated by the experience of Soviet weightlifter Vasily Alexeyev. In 1976 no one had ever lifted 500 pounds, and Vasily could not break that barrier. His trainers overcame this limit by telling him that a bar weighed 499.9 pounds, revealing only after he lifted it that it actually weighed 501 ½ pounds. Once he'd broken his own 500-pound limit, Alexeyev was able to go on to lift 564 pounds.[10]

The following exercise (taken from Aikido) will give you and your students an opportunity to experience the effect of mind set on performance.

EXERCISE 1

Stand facing a student with your arm extended to the side. Tell the student that in a minute he is to walk briskly toward your arm and try not to let it stop him. Before he begins, have him think about a spot behind him and concentrate on that spot as he walks. His body is to move forward but his mind is to be behind him. Your arm should be firm enough so that it is not easily moved. Repeat the exercise with the same student, but this time tell him to walk just as he did before but to concentrate on a spot beyond your arm so that both body and mind are moving forward. Let several students try the exercise; then discuss their experiences and how you felt their strength both times. Have the class divide into pairs so that everyone has a chance to experience the difference for themselves.

In doing this exercise, students should experience that they move much more powerfully when their minds are forward. The change in performance comes not from what they do but from the way their minds affect what they do. You can follow the exercise with a discussion of the effects of mental attitude on performance in all areas and applied specifically to the subjects you're teaching. Most students have had experience with doing very well at something until they think about it ("Look how well I'm typing; I haven't made a mistake . . . Oops."); their minds slip backward, and they make the mistake. After the discussion, a simple command of "Mind forward" will remind students to focus attention consciously, though it will take practice to make that become a consistent part of their approach.

Optimal performance training focuses very specifically on creating a positive mental set. Athletes go through relaxation exercises similar to the one in Chapter 6. In a deeply relaxed state the mind is more open to suggestion, and the athletes repeat to themselves affirmations like "I feel relaxed and confident as I wait for the ball" and "I hit the ball every time with ease." At the same time they imagine as vividly as possible that they are experiencing what they affirm. They see and feel themselves performing with confidence and ease—shooting the perfect basket or gracefully executing a difficult dance step. The same technique can be used for any skill—for example, in typing, "I type _____ wpm without errors," or in driving, "I shift gears smoothly and easily." The exercises on pages 139–40 of Chapter 6 use this technique to prepare students for studying and test taking.

Imagery rehearsal goes a step beyond affirmation; in a state of deep relaxation, athletes imagine themselves practicing a movement sequence. In their minds they go through an entire ski run flawlessly or practice shooting baskets or hitting a tennis ball. If they feel themselves making an error, they begin again and repeat the practice. We don't know how image rehearsal has the effect it does, but some researchers have hypothesized that the brain does not easily distinguish between vivid multisensory imagery and actual practice, causing imagery to have much the same effect as action. Of course, athletes must have a clear sense of how the correct motion feels and must be able to generate clear visual and kinesthetic imagery so that they create the experience fully in their minds.

Imagery rehearsal may be too advanced a technique for most teachers, but developing kinesthetic awareness and using relaxation and affirmation exercises can be useful in a wide range of subjects. In learning these skills, students not only will improve their performance in a given area but will gain valuable tools which can be applied in many ways both in school and beyond.

SMELL AND TASTE

Compared to kinesthetic and tactile perception, smell and taste play so small a role in most subjects that one might be tempted to dismiss them, but there are cases where they're important. Smell is a powerful trigger to memory and a key to rich associations of experience and emotion. It should be a part of any fantasy as it deepens and personalizes involvement. You'll notice that some students respond to and generate smell imagery more easily than others. The ability to identify and discriminate between smells plays a role in certain subjects; for example, chemistry teachers frequently smell solutions to get information about them. They should suggest that students use the same technique and help them develop a vocabulary to identify and remember different odors. In cooking, smell and taste convey important information which teachers should explicitly make students aware of.

In writing, the ability to describe all types of sensations vividly is an important skill. Teachers can develop sensory awareness and vocabulary through experiences which stimulate the senses. One such exercise is to have students encounter different substances blindfolded or with their eyes closed, relying solely on smell, taste, or touch. Ask them to find words to describe each substance—not to guess its identity but to describe its qualities. The words can be shared and discussed; once they are clarified and understood, they can be used in poetry or prose assignments. A similar exercise can be used to stimulate memories for a creative writing assignment.

Teachers who work with learning disabled students often use a multisensory approach because their students may need information presented through as many channels as possible. While most of their work is with the tactile-kinesthetic systems, they sometimes use cereal letters so that a child can eat a word if he reads or spells it correctly. They may use raisins or peanuts to illustrate math concepts or to spell words. The food acts as a motivator and may also help make associative links. Pens with special odors and colors or scented shaving cream can be used to involve the sense of smell in making connections. It is also possible that they increase the arousal level in the child and help focus attention on the task.

NONVERBAL AUDITORY LEARNING (MUSIC)

Music, like art, is an important part of human experience and should therefore be part of education for its own sake. However, the applications we will discuss in this book will be limited to the role of music in learning substantive material. Research with stroke victims indicates that songs actually bridge the hemispheres—that is, the right hemisphere learns the melody while the left learns the words. Therapists find that some patients who've lost the ability to talk can learn to speak and remember simple phrases when the phrases are set to musical fragments.[11] This finding suggests that when students learn verbal information with a song, they may have an extra aid in recalling it. It's important to realize that the music helps in retention, not in comprehension. However, there are many situations, especially in the primary grades, where students need to memorize information, such as math facts, spelling, or certain dates. Singing can make a tedious task enjoyable, thus keeping students' attention and interest. Teachers who are willing to make up simple tunes or adapt familiar ones to their uses can combine music with whatever else they want to teach.

The Orff-Schulwerk philosophy of music education, which is used widely in the schools of Europe, provides a methodology for teaching music, for using it to teach other subjects such as spelling and math, and for developing creative capacity. Orff works with a simple five-tone scale within which there are no possible combinations of notes that are displeasing to the ear. The scale enables even young children to improvise and compose pleasing melodies. Students also explore and improvise with different rhythmic patterns through clapping and movement. Orff emphasizes improvisation, encouraging children to create and play with their own compositions rather than teaching them standard songs. This type of activity not only teaches students a great deal about music and movement, it develops problem-solving and creative capacities. In addition, it is fun and stimulates participation from many students who withdraw from other school experiences. The Orff-Schulwerk Association offers workshops around the United States.[12]

Music is a part of any historical period; its inclusion in a history class provides an added dimension. It also offers another context, just as art and architecture do, within which to explore the themes and attitudes of a period and to make comparisons with other periods. As an example, one can ask students to compare Baroque and Classic music in terms of what they know of the two periods. Even musically unsophisticated students can sense differences in the two types of music and make connections to their knowledge of the historical periods.

Folk music has always reflected the lives of the people who wrote it and can enliven and enrich history classes. Songs often reveal the issues, events, and dreams of social movements with an immediacy lacking in facts and dates. They stimulate emotional involvement and capture the imagination. Songs such as "Follow the Drinking Gourd," "John Henry," and "So Long, It's Been Good to Know You" offer students human voices commenting on their times and circumstances. Students may remember points made in connection with the songs that they would not retain from a textbook.

In foreign language classes, learning songs is an enjoyable way to build vocabulary, learn new patterns, and develop fluency. The melodies you use should be familiar to the students so that they are not distracted by learning both a new tune and lyrics in a foreign language. If you make up new lyrics to go with a familiar tune, you can tailor your songs to teach whatever structures or vocabulary you wish.

A Bulgarian physicist, Dr. Georgi Lozanov, uses music to teach foreign languages in quite a different way, and his work offers exciting possibilities for music to play a new role in learning for all ages and many subjects. Lozanov has devised a method he calls *Suggestology,* which he reports enables students to learn much more material in less time with less effort. In Lozanov's foreign language classes students acquire a 2,000-word vocabulary in eighty-four hours of instruction (3½ hours a day, six days a week, for four weeks). U. S. Department of State and military language classes using intensive audiolingual training require 300 hours of instruction in Romance languages to achieve a 2 + level in the Foreign Service Institute speaking proficiency scale. Lozanov's classes in English achieve this level with 84 hours of instruction. When used with tenth-grade students in foreign language classes, the method reduced the daily student workload by two hours in school and four at home; it also enabled students to finish the nine-month curriculum in seven months.[13]

Lozanov's method is based on the premise that the mind is capable of learning many times more efficiently than we usually assume when self-imposed barriers are eliminated and an optimal environment is created. Every aspect of the classroom and the teacher's presentation is designed to create an atmosphere that gives students confidence in their own abilities and minimizes both external and internal distractions. In this method, music is one of the principal tools for inducing a mental state in which material is more easily absorbed and retained. The music is played while students relax and listen to the teacher act out the lesson dialogue. Students do not concentrate on the words but enter a receptive state in which the teacher's words may suggest images and the dialogue is absorbed without conscious effort. Lozanov uses music written in 4/4 time played at a slow tempo of 60 beats per minute, because it is believed that such music lulls the mind into a receptive state where it is fully relaxed yet also alert and open to stimuli. Electroencephalogram tests have demonstrated that the brain responds to music with altered brain waves;[14] Lozanov uses this quality to induce both mind and body to relax while remaining receptive.

Interest in *Suggestology* within Bulgaria and from the rest of the world has enabled Lozanov to expand his research with the method. It is currently being used to teach basic skills in the primary grades, and preliminary reports indicate great success. The method involves a great deal more than has been presented in this brief discussion; it is a carefully sequenced and orchestrated approach to learning. It would be a mistake to try to adopt one part of it without an understanding of the whole. However, for those willing to study his method, Lozanov's work suggests a powerful new role for music in learning.

NOTES

1. RAYMOND S. MORE, DOROTHY N. MORE, et al., *School Can Wait* (Provo, Utah: Brigham Young University Press, 1979), p. 153.
2. For directions for such games see HANS G. FURTH and HARRY WACHS, *Thinking Goes to School* (New York: Oxford University Press, 1975).
3. Ibid., p. 74.
4. Many districts have specialists to whom children can be referred for testing. Some pediatricians, hospitals, and independent therapists are also trained to do evaluations. The quality of both school and community resources varies widely; parents and teachers are advised to select carefully.
5. From R. H. McKIM, *Experiences in Visual Thinking* (Monterey, Calif.: Brooks/Cole, 1972), p. 40, reprinted by permission of the publisher. Copyright © 1972, by Wadsworth Publishing Company.
6. From PATRICIA S. DAVIDSON, "Exploring the Neuropsychology of Math," a workshop presented by the California Association of Neurologically Handicapped Children—An Association for Children and Adults with Learning Disabilities (CANHC-ACLD), San Francisco, Calif., February 1982.
7. JOYCE BOORMAN, *Dance and Language Experiences with*

Children (Don Mills, Ont., Canada: Longman Canada Ltd, 1974), p. 12.

8. Ibid.

9. THOMAS TUTKO and UMBERTO TOSI, *Sports Psyching: Playing Your Best Game All of the Time* (Los Angeles, Calif.: J. P. Tarcher, 1980), p. 155.

10. SHEILA OSTRANDER and LYNN SCHROEDER with NANCY OSTRANDER, *Superlearning* (New York: Delta/Confucian Press, 1980), p. 157.

11. HOWARD GARDINER, *The Shattered Mind* (New York: Knopf, 1975), pp. 344–48.

12. For information on Orff-Schulwerk workshops, write American Orff-Schulwerk Association (AOSA), Dept. of Music, Cleveland State University, Cleveland, Ohio 44115.

13. ALLYN PRICHARD and JEAN TAYLOR, *Accelerating Learning: The Use of Suggestion in the Classroom* (Novato, Calif.: Academic Therapy Publications, 1980), pp. 16–17.

14. OSTRANDER and SCHROEDER, *Superlearning*, p. 72.

DIRECT
EXPERIENCE

Long before researchers began to explore the mysteries of the two hemispheres, teachers knew the importance of experience in the learning process. Today, with limited financial resources and pressure to produce results on proficiency tests, teachers are increasingly forced to justify the extra time and expense required for experiential learning. The research on the hemispheres suggests several reasons that experience should be an important part of any learning situation.

We've seen that the difference between gestalt perception (seeing the whole) and feature detection (finding the parts) seems to be basic to the different modes of processing of the hemispheres. Textbooks and lectures are usually organized in a linear fashion. Experiential learning, on the other hand, provides students with a meaningful whole, a total situation, and challenges them to discover its parts and their relationships to each other. For students who are not verbally oriented or who need a sense of the whole before they attack the parts, experiential learning is much more likely to bring success.

Even for highly verbal students direct experience is essential for the development of important cognitive skills. A book, no matter how good, cannot provide the same learning as direct experience. It presents the brain with a different type of stimulus. The world we live in is not ordered and arranged in the neat categories of a textbook. It presents us with a vast amount of information which we must order for ourselves and from which we must find ways of making meaning. Experiential learning stimulates original thinking and develops a wide range of thinking strategies and perceptual skills which are not called forth by books or lectures.

Experiential learning has another quality that is important for all students but especially for those whose motivation for academic tasks is low. It has the capacity to stimulate more personal involvement and thus draw these students into a subject they might otherwise avoid.

Finally, as we've seen in Chapter 7, experience is absolutely essential for the learning of young children. They must encounter phenomena with their senses, must be able to explore and manipulate them. We can give them words, but words alone do not create understanding.

In this chapter we'll look at several ways of providing experience-based learning. Field trips, laboratory experiments, the use of real objects and primary source material all offer opportunities for direct interaction with the phenomena being studied. Simulation and role playing place the students in a situation and let them create the experience for themselves. These techniques are familiar to most teachers. They are used in so many different and innovative ways that to treat them fully would require far more space than this book allows. However, a few examples will suggest the possibilities offered by each technique.

LABORATORY
EXPERIMENTS

The word *laboratory* conjures the image of an expensively outfitted single-purpose room. Yet a great deal can be done in a regular classroom with inexpensive materials. A lab is a place to experiment with real things. For young children the whole world is a laboratory. They experiment with social relations on the playground; they test objects to see how far they can be thrown, what they're good for, and so on. In fact, the classroom is often the place we allow them the least opportunity to function as scientists because we require that they accept and learn what the teacher and the book say is so.

Elementary teachers who have access to SCIIS (Science Curriculum Improvement Study) materials have not only excellent science courses to teach but a model for how to guide students through scientific investigations. Students are not told what they're supposed to learn. They're given real materials to manipulate and observe, and through their observations, they discover information. The focus is on the process on how one does science as well as the concepts and information to be learned. Even if one is not using the SCIIS kits, their teaching manuals provide invaluable guidance on how to approach the teaching of science.

Materials for science study are all around us; by using common materials, you give students the opportunity to repeat experiments at home. The books in the Brown Paper School series offer a number of experiments that use easily available materials. Other resources for low-cost science teaching are included in the Bibliography.

If we want students to be interested in science and find it stimulating and rewarding enough to do the hard work it requires, we must pay more attention to the science experiences we provide in elementary school. The effort to save money by substituting books for real materials in the early years is costly in the long run.

Zoc Ipsen of Oxford School in Berkeley, California, does a unit on embryology with her third graders. She puts twenty-four eggs in an incubator and every three days she and the students open an egg, examine its contents, and preserve the embryo in a pickling jar. She leaves some eggs to hatch into chicks. No book could create the excitement and involvement, the development of observational skills, or the introduction to scientific investigation that this unit produces.

Junior and senior high school science teachers usually have laboratory facilities, but facilities and materials do not guarantee effective teaching. If students are doing experiments to get the "right" results, they are more likely to be coping than thinking. They are simply demonstrating information from the laboratory manual. Scientists do not know what results an experiment will yield; they watch and try to make sense of the results. Students can do the same, but only if the emphasis is on the process ("Why do you think it turned out that way?") instead of the information ("That's not right. Do it again.").

FIELD TRIPS

Field trips offer tremendous opportunities for learning, but they too seldom realize this potential. A successful field trip requires planning; the teacher must have clear instructional goals and structured ways of achieving those goals. To simply take a group of students to a museum or a beach and assume they'll learn something is not enough. Without proper preparation and guidance in how to approach the experience most students will be overwhelmed and unable to focus their attention. Few students have the self-discipline to devise their own structure.

Before the field trip, the teacher should decide on the main goals it is to accomplish. What do you want students to learn? What should they pay attention to? What preparation will they need to appreciate the significance of what they're seeing? One approach for older students is to provide a written guide that directs them to different points and asks them to observe specific things or answer specific questions. Another is to make a game of the experience. Set up a "treasure hunt" by asking students to find one example of X (a mollusk, a Renaissance portrait, an animal that crawls), two examples of Y, and so forth.

Field trips can be a good opportunity for practical problem-solving experience, even for elementary students. Marjorie Musante gave her fourth graders at Sleepy Hollow School, Orinda, California, the responsibility for arranging their own field trip— an overnight stay on the *C. A. Thayer*, a nineteenth-century lumbering and codfishing ship at the San Francisco Maritime Museum (her experience is described more fully in the section on "Simulation" in this chapter). The children made phone calls, wrote letters, earned money, arranged for transportation, and tackled all the practical problems posed by the trip. Involving students in such a planning process teaches valuable practical planning skills and offers a real world opportunity to apply language and math.

Field trips need not require a bus to take you across town. For elementary students a visit to the firehouse or the grocery store can provide rich opportunities for learning. Investigate the resources within walking distance from your school. A vacant lot full of weeds can offer enough material for a number of science lessons for students of any age. One high school biology class did a year-long study of the ecosystem in the field at the edge of their schoolyard. Another teacher converted a dirt area near the parking lot into an archeological dig for his class by burying cheap, everyday objects and having students recover them and speculate as to their meaning in the culture.

In Berkeley, California, Trish Hawthorne is working with teachers to develop a unit on history and architecture for elementary grades. The unit begins with the history of the children's school—old pictures and descriptions of their experiences by people who were students in the school's early years—to give children a sense of life in the past. The basic architectural concepts are taught with photographs and slides of houses and buildings in the community, and the unit culminates with a walking tour through the neighborhood. The children are given maps and directions to find certain things on specific houses, so the experience is structured both to cement their understanding of the architectural concepts and to develop their powers of observation. History and architecture come together in familiar places and buildings seen in a new way.

REAL OBJECTS AND PRIMARY SOURCE MATERIAL

A bone found on the way to school, an arrowhead from grandfather's house, souvenirs brought back from a vacation in another country—all these objects have educational value if we use them. Real objects are concrete, and some students need the concrete to learn. Talking or reading about a subject does not capture their attention and motivate them. If you decide to set aside time for discussion of objects students bring, it's best to structure the experience by setting a category, such as "something from the past" or "a tool" or "something a student made." Investigation and discussion of the objects provide practice in oral language and stimulate questions and interests which may be used in future activities.

Parents are an excellent source of real objects. Send home a questionnaire to find out what resources they can provide. Do they have objects from foreign countries, from their work, from their family's past? Your local historical society may have a collection of objects and old photos that they'll bring to show your class. No matter what you're teaching, ask yourself how you can get objects to make the lesson more concrete, more grounded in experience.

Primary Sources. Written primary source material does not have quite the immediacy of real objects, but it is a good deal more experiential than a textbook presentation. In the study of history, diaries, letters, newspaper articles, photos, art, music, and literature help create a sense of time and place. They are more personal and evocative than the objective language of a textbook. They present concrete examples from real lives and suggest images and feelings. These qualities have power to involve and motivate some students who do not respond to the treatment of history in a textbook.

Primary source material, like all forms of direct experience, offers a rich variety of information, but that information is not organized around the concepts and specific points of a history text. Students may require some help in extracting the historical significance of primary sources. Questions like, "How did the writer feel about the war?" "Was that attitude representative of the feelings of most other people at that time?" can challenge students to make connections between source material and themes explored in class.

Each child has a personal history—that is, a family that came from somewhere at some time. If you can get students to bring their families' stories into the classroom, you have not only a rich source of information but a high level of involvement. Starting a year or a unit with family histories can set the stage for the entire course. Find a way to represent where the ancestors of each child were during each historical period; then as you teach about that period refer back to the ancestors. They can become concrete examples for many different points. You will also be demonstrating that history is not a list of dates and facts but the unfolding process that has brought each of us to where we are today.

SIMULATION

Simulation is a technique for creating experience through which students can learn about a subject. The teacher designs a situation which is analogous in significant ways to the phenomenon being taught and assigns students roles. Rules are established which allow students to experience the constraints inherent in the situation and to gain insight into the subject.

Simulation and role playing are similar in many ways, and understanding the differences between the two is less important than exploring their use in the teaching process. Both techniques can be used for a number of the same purposes; they can help in studying specific subjects, in practicing problem-solving strategies, and in developing self-awareness and interpersonal skills. One difference between the two is that in simulation the students do not become someone else. The roles they play in the simulation are determined by their own reactions to the constraints and opportunities the situation offers. They do not imagine how some other person would respond as they would in role playing. If you set up a town meeting in Germany in 1940 and assign students to play the roles of different individuals such as a shopkeeper, a soldier, or a factory owner, that is role playing. If you set up a situation in which you create conditions similar to those existing in Nazi Germany and operate the classroom under those rules, that is a simulation.

Simulations are most commonly associated with social studies, and a number of commercially developed games are available. However, simulation as a teaching technique is applicable to any subject; teachers can often design exercises better tailored to their classes' needs and more appropriate to specific teaching goals than commercial products. Simulation can be used in all subjects from a social studies class exploring issues of power to a science class examining how atoms bond to form simple molecules. One can simulate a visit to a French café for a foreign language class, requiring students to express themselves in French as would be necessary in Paris. Simulation can even be used to integrate several subjects at once.

Marjorie Musante, who teaches fourth grade at Sleepy Hollow School in Orinda, California, uses a major theme around which she organizes her teaching for the year. One year she chose ships as the theme and turned her classroom into a ship. Windows were converted to portholes, a ship's bell was used to ring ship's time, and ship's flags communicated messages like "Quiet." Vocabulary and spelling lessons included nautical terms (spelling was optional, but most students chose to do it and scored better than on the easier list of standard words). The students learned to tie knots and sew ditty bags (good for eye–hand coordination, following directions, and small muscle control). Reading, math, and writing assignments were designed to fit the theme, and in history students studied the role of shipping in the growth of California. An entry was made in the class ship's log to record the events of each day. For many students, this type of integrated learning experience in which many different activities are linked together by a common theme produces added motivation which enables them to apply themselves in areas they might otherwise resist.

Using the National Maritime Museum Environmental Living Program, Ms. Musante was able to give her students the experience of life on a sailing ship in the 1930s. The class spent a weekend on the *C. A. Thayer,* a restored lumber and codfishing schooner docked at the San Francisco Maritime Museum. The experience was structured so that the students were limited to the technology available on that ship in the 1930s; they had no refrigeration, and food was cooked on the *Thayer*'s wood-burning stove. The students were divided into crews and worked at the tasks sailors performed—raising sail, fishing in a dory, swabbing decks, and standing watch through the night. The results were not only a much greater understanding of life in an earlier time but also increased self-confidence and a feeling of community among the students.

Mitch Backiel of Mt. Greylock High School in Massachusetts designed a simulation to help his biology class understand molecular bonding. He assigned each student to be an atom of hydrogen, oxygen, carbon, or nitrogen. Hydrogen atoms could only form one bond, so hydrogen students could only use one arm to form a bond, oxygen students could use both arms, and carbon students could use both arms and legs to form bonds. The students were then told to find and bond with other students with whom they might form molecules or organic compounds.

In high school civics, Ron Jones of Cubberly High School in Palo Alto, California, wanted to extend his students' understanding of the differences between capitalism, socialism, communism, and anarchy. He divided the class into four groups, with each group representing a different system, and assigned the groups to plan a lunch which would be consistent with their group's principles and manner of operating. The capitalists were to demonstrate their understanding of capitalism by the way they set up the "capitalist lunch." Each of the other groups was to do the same with its identification. After lunch, students discussed what they'd done and what it reflected about their assigned system. They explored the strengths and weaknesses of each system in terms of their experience.

ROLE PLAYING

Role playing, like simulation, creates an experience in the classroom. In role playing, the students take the part of other people and try to act as those people would in a given situation. The students must imagine how the people would feel and behave. In many cases, they must know quite a bit about the people whose roles they are playing in order to do an effective job.

In her European literature class, Connie Woulf of Albany

High School, Albany, California, has students play "The Dating Game" (patterned after the television program). The bachelors are Petrarch, Boccaccio, and Siegfried. The boys are assigned roles; the girls prepare questions. The class also conducts interviews for the position of principal of their high school. In one class, the applicants were Roland, Machiavelli, and Dr. Panglos (from *Candide*). Students volunteer for each of these roles, and an interview committee draws up a set of questions. The rest of the class can also ask questions, and they evaluate the quality and consistency of the interviewees' answers. The entire class votes to select the successful candidate.

It sounds like great fun, and it is; but it is also a learning experience. To prepare for the dating game, the boys must really understand the different attitudes of each character. Statements memorized from books and lectures won't help them answer "What's your idea of the perfect date?" The girls must also understand the difference between the characters to evaluate their responses, and they must figure out what questions will identify the essence of the different attitudes. The interviews for principal force students to focus on questions of power and governance as well as clarifying how the different characters stand on those issues. In a class that feels more like a game than a lesson, these students do a great deal of higher-level thinking; they integrate information from different historical periods to see relationships and changes over time. They use information instead of simply storing it and repeating it back. Later, as they write papers or answer essay questions on a test, their increased understanding is demonstrated in the quality of their written work.

In her regular English II classes, Ms. Woulf has students play "To Tell the Truth" (another television game show) with characters from *The Taming of the Shrew* and *Animal Farm*. Three students are assigned to be a given character, such as Boxer or Squealer from *Animal Farm*. They must respond to questions, the answers to which are often not in the book. The class votes on which student did the most convincing job, and that student earns bonus points. Ms. Woulf points out that often students demonstrate an impressive understanding of their character which goes far beyond their ability to express themselves in writing.

Trials are another popular role-playing situation. One can role-play a real trial like that of Copernicus or the Scopes trial; or one can invent a trial, such as one with Macbeth as the defendant. Students playing the roles are challenged to achieve an in-depth understanding of the material and the rest of the class is offered an enjoyable and involving review session.

CONCLUSION

If you ask a group of adults what learning experience they remember from their years as students, the answers will usually involve two things—some form of direct experience and a moment of insight or discovery. Often the two occur together, with the experience leading to the insight. The types of learning experiences described in this chapter have the power to command a place in memory not just because they are fun but because they stimulate students to think and make meaning for themselves. This type of mental challenge is pleasurable; it contributes to self-esteem and makes learning a self-reinforcing activity.

9

HOW
TO START

The first thing to realize is that you've already started. If you've read this far, you've invested time and thought in right-hemisphere teaching. In addition, you've probably also discovered that you're already using some of the techniques described as right hemisphere. So you're on your way.

The next thing to realize is that if you really want to make more conscious use of the techniques in this book, it will require an effort over time. It's easy enough to talk about using more visual strategies, but if your current style doesn't include that, it's apt to take more than good intentions to make drawing a consistent part of your teaching.

Teaching style, like learning style, is an individual matter, and the way one goes about making changes is part of that style. If you are to be successful at making basic changes, you'll need to be clear on your goals and on how you plan to achieve them. Think back and identify times in the past when you've wanted to do something new. How have you gone about it? Identify both times you've succeeded and times you've failed, and figure out how your strategy differed in the two cases. In short, become aware of the process that enables *you* to be most successful in making changes and mastering new skills. With that in mind you can consider the process suggested in this chapter and either use it or modify it to meet your needs.

Excitement and enthusiasm are great allies in making changes. However, they can backfire if they lead you to try everything at once—to rush in Monday morning with a fantasy or a complex simulation. That plunge-right-in approach can lead to frustration and failure for both you and your students that will sap the energy needed for long-range change. The process of changing anything so basic as one's teaching style is a slow process that occurs over time. It's important to realize that small changes made consistently over a year can amount to a major change that is much more likely to be lasting than a few "big" projects.

A Few Rules
Go at your own pace.
Do what you enjoy.
Give yourself every chance for success.
Start with your strengths.

PLANNING FOR CHANGE

You're no doubt already using some of the techniques in this book to some extent. You offer metaphors when they suggest themselves, make simple charts or drawings on the board, do some role playing or simulation. Become aware of what you're *already* doing and make those right-hemisphere strategies a conscious and explicit part of your teaching process. If you use metaphor occasionally, consciously generate metaphors as part of your lesson planning and begin to ask students to offer *their* metaphors in class. If you doodle or draw on the board, expand your use of that strategy and encourage students to represent their ideas visually for you.

By beginning with the techniques that come most easily for you, you allow yourself to experiment and learn in a way that's pleasant and easy, and the experience you gain will help you master the techniques that come less naturally. It may help to rate the techniques as *A, B,* or *C* for yourself—*A* for those you can use right now, *B* for those that seem a bit more difficult to integrate into your teaching style, and *C* for those that you'll want more experience with or training in before you try to use them.

Start with a technique in your *A* group and make it a conscious part of your lesson planning. Make a commitment to use it at least once a week in one class. Devote some time to planning that part of the lesson, and take time afterward to evaluate how it worked. Keep a journal of your experience, evaluations, and ideas for modifications. If you do nothing more than this, by the end of the school year you will have developed about thirty new lessons.

Once you feel competent with one technique, add another and use both until you feel comfortable with them. You can add techniques at whatever rate is appropriate for you, but be sure you continue to use the ones you've already introduced. They will become a part of your teaching style only if you use them regularly.

As you're beginning to use one or more of the techniques from your *A* group, you can begin to think of ways to gain experience with a technique in your *C* group. You can select a book from the Bibliography. You can find one or more teachers in your district who use the technique and observe them (this is one of the best ways to learn a new technique since it gives you a model, and it's much easier to learn to do something if you've watched someone else do it well). You can also convince the district to organize an in-service program in the area that interests you, or look for a class or workshop at a local educational institution. There are numerous ways to start; select one that appeals to you, but do something while you have the enthusiasm to get started. Don't put it off.

The techniques in this book will be most effective when they become a consistent part of your everyday teaching. That won't happen at once, but it should be your long-range goal. If you decide to adopt a two-sided approach to teaching, another long-range goal will be to plan whole units to include both right- and left-hemisphere techniques. One way to do this is to view the teaching process as divided into three phases—information is taken in, it's processed, and students express their understanding of it in some way. Each of these three phases should include both "right" and "left" processes. In planning you can divide a unit into those three parts and consciously balance methods of presentation, activities that aid comprehension, and forms of evaluation.

It's important not only that you use both types of technique but also that you ask students to use them. The diagram you draw for students may clarify the concept for them, but the ones they draw for you will help make that concept truly theirs. Asking students to develop metaphors, visual materials, or simple simulations to present to the class is an excellent way of reviewing material. The students who've mastered the material deepen their own comprehension by presenting it for others, and the rest of the class gets a helpful review (to insure that the review is helpful, have the students go over their presentation with you before they do it for the class so you can clear up anything that might create confusion). When dealing with the evaluation phase, you may not be able to change your form of evaluation. Nevertheless, before the test you can allow students an opportunity to express their understanding in a variety of ways. The more ways they explore a concept, the better they will understand it.

STARTING NOW

One change you can make right now that will help structure further change is to redesign the form of your lesson plan so that it serves as a reminder to encourage new ideas. Find a way to make a "two-sided" lesson plan. Make space for right-hemisphere goals and techniques; you may not always have something to put in those spaces, but their presence will remind you of possibilities you might otherwise overlook.

Another thing you can start to do now is to study your students' learning styles. Select one student and set aside three to five minutes each day to observe him informally. Watch as he solves different problems and try to see how his mind approaches different tasks. Keep notes on your observations. Next week observe another student the same way. Talk with students about how they work; sit beside them and have them talk their way through a task. Some students will find this easy, while others will find it very difficult. If they have trouble verbalizing, just watch and, if necessary, ask questions. Be very careful not to put a student on the spot. Low achievers may be made especially sensitive and uncomfortable by your attention.

Enlist your students in your explorations. Tell them about learning styles and encourage them to share their experiences and perceptions with you. Even elementary students can become excited by such discussion because the subject is one that is of great personal interest to them. In doing this, you'll help your students begin to develop an awareness of their own strategies and modes of thinking.

Helping students understand their own learning styles is especially important for students with learning disabilities and those who do not succeed easily with traditional approaches. They may not always be fortunate enough to have a teacher who recognizes their individual needs. You can help them greatly by making them aware of their learning style, how to use its strengths, and how to ask for the kind of help they need.

Another area in which you can begin work is strengthening the capabilities which are underdeveloped in each student. One approach is to help them translate from one medium to another. If they are weak in verbal processing but good in visual thinking, encourage them to use visual strategies to clarify their ideas and to plan written work. If they do well on verbal assignments but are confused by diagrams and other forms of graphic representation, have them talk their way through decoding diagrams and graphs.

INTANGIBLES

Teaching is full of intangibles—factors like trust, expectations, and motivation that can't be measured but that play a crucial role in the process. In introducing new techniques they become even more important.

Trust. The greater the degree of trust between teacher and students, the more easily and effectively new techniques can be introduced. Students, like everyone else, like to feel that they are liked and respected and that someone cares about them; they dislike being ridiculed or rejected. The extent to which they will risk trying new skills and new ways of approaching problems depends to a large degree on how much they trust the teacher to be supportive of their efforts and to protect them from ridicule and rejection.

Expectations. Students' beliefs about their own competence have a tremendous effect on their performance, and their self-esteem is heavily influenced by their teachers' attitudes. The effect of teachers' expectations was demonstrated in an experiment where teachers were told that certain students were performing beneath their ability level and would show dramatic improvement in the next three months. The students were randomly selected, and the experimenter had no reason to expect them to improve. However, by the end of the experiment, the students whom teachers expected to improve had, in fact, improved. The only factor that could explain their improvement was the change in the teachers' expectations.[1]

One advantage of introducing new techniques is that they offer a chance to succeed to some students who've been unsuccessful with other approaches. When you introduce right-hemisphere techniques, expect students to do well with them and communicate that expectation to the class. Expect to be surprised by several students' improvement, and you probably will be. Since facility with linear, verbal approaches is not necessary for success with right-hemisphere techniques, previous performance is no indicator of how well students will do.

Motivation. One important feature of the techniques in this book is that students enjoy them; they seem to make schoolwork more fun. When learning is pleasurable, it creates motivation, and motivation in turn makes learning more efficient. In an article in the *Journal of Learning Disabilities,* Marianne Frostig and Phyllis Maslow of the Frostig Center of Educational Therapy in

Los Angeles point out that animal research demonstrates that cortical (higher brain) impulses are amplified two or three times by motivation. They also cite research showing that stimulation of the brain's pleasure centers produces a high level of motivation.[2] This research demonstrates what teachers have always known—that wanting to learn something makes it more possible to learn and that efforts to make learning pleasurable have a direct and positive effect on learning efficiency. At a time when pressure to go "back to basics" sometimes promotes suspicion of learning approaches that are fun for students, this research becomes particularly relevant.

REDISCOVERING YOUR SUBJECT

Many teachers who begin to use the techniques described in this book in their teaching find themselves rediscovering their subjects. The techniques encourage students to ask questions which go beyond the information in the text, questions which are creative and interesting but which the teacher may not have ready answers for. While this situation may be disconcerting at first, it is a sign of how much more stimulating the class has become. It demonstrates that students are thinking independently about the subject and not simply memorizing facts for a test.

Teachers who use these techniques will have to answer, "I don't know" to many more questions than ones who work exclusively from a text. They may also find themselves doing more research into their subjects for a couple of years, but this situation has its benefits. A subject which may have become "old hat" and rather dull can come alive and stimulate new learning if students' questions are seen as a challenge rather than a burden. To handle new questions, it may help to identify books which can give students information that goes beyond the text so that you can do some of the research together or they can do it for themselves. Be careful not to *require* students to find the answers to their questions; that is a sure way to discourage questions.

PERSONAL GROWTH

This book has focused on the benefits to students of a two-sided approach, but right-hemisphere techniques have something to offer teachers as well. We are products of a system that emphasized linear, verbal processes, and many of us have missed the opportunity to develop some of our right-hemisphere capabilities. Fortunately, those basic powers of the mind are not lost by disuse. They can be reclaimed at any time. If you don't know how to draw or visualize or use metaphor, you can still learn, and in learning, you can discover a great source of growth and pleasure. The marvelous abilities of the right and left hemispheres belong to all of us, but they only become accessible if we use them. In teaching yourself to use right-hemisphere techniques, you will develop new capabilities within yourself as well as within your students.

WORKING TOGETHER

Expanding your teaching style is easier if you find colleagues to help. You don't need to be all things to all students; you can find another teacher to cover areas where you lack experience. One second-grade teacher who's a math specialist trades classes with a kindergarten teacher who loves music, so that each class has the benefit of two teachers' expertise several times a week. A high school English teacher does poetry with the art class twice a month while the art teacher helps her class with art projects associated with their reading. A music teacher advises a history teacher on music of different historical periods.

With your awareness of right-hemisphere strategies, look at the resources your fellow faculty members have to offer. Is there a physical education teacher who teaches yoga or relaxation techniques? Is there someone already using mind mapping? Are the students especially enthusiastic about someone's field trips? Talk about the ideas in this book and listen for responses that show interest or expertise. You may find someone who's studied yoga who will teach you some breathing exercises to help students relax and concentrate, or someone who knows of a workshop on a topic that interests you.

Anyone in your school or district office who is trained in learning disabilities or special education is likely to be an excellent resource. Learning disability specialists are usually familiar with hemispheric research; they are also astute observers of the learning process, and they're trained to teach through all the sensory modalities. They can often offer insights into the learning problems of specific students, and they possess a rich repertoire of teaching strategies directed to both hemispheres.

SUPPORT GROUPS

Any time you want to make changes, a support group can be very helpful. A group generates energy; it offers a forum for exploring and refining ideas for new activities and provides an outside impetus to keep you moving when you're tempted to give up. Identify others on your faculty or in your district who might share your interest in expanding their teaching styles. Once you have several people willing to commit themselves to the group, arrange a regular meeting time. Once a week go over each person's goals, what they've done that week, and what they are thinking of doing the next week. It's harder to put off something if you know you'll be asked about it at the next meeting, and it's more fun to plan if you have others' ideas to stimulate your own.

There are advantages to having people with different backgrounds in your group. A home economics teacher may have a fresh approach to the problems of teaching French. An English teacher who isn't familiar with physics concepts can force you to clarify confusing material so it's more comprehensible to students. People from the same discipline often share a common point of view; working with a diverse group gives you a richer variety of ideas.

CONCLUSION

Children come to school as integrated people with thoughts and feelings, words and pictures, ideas and fantasies. They are intensely curious about the world. They are scientists, artists, musicians, historians, dancers and runners, tellers of stories, and mathematicians. The challenge we face as teachers is to use the wealth they bring us. They come with a two-sided mind. We must encourage them to use it, to develop both types of thinking so that they have access to the fullest possible range of mental abilities.

NOTES

1. ROBERT ROSENTHAL, "The Pygmalion Effect Lives," *Psychology Today,* 7, no. 4 (September 1973).
2. MARIANNE FROSTIG and PHYLLIS MASLOW, "Neuropsychological Contributions to Education," *Journal of Learning Disabilities,* 12, no. 8 (October 1979), pp. 40–54.

10

CONCLUSION

We began this book with a hypothetical two-sided lesson in science, and we proceeded to look at each of the techniques one by one. At this point you may be in the position of a student who's been given too many parts and is losing track of the whole picture. To return to the larger picture and to try to put the parts within a meaningful whole, let's take a stroll down the hall of a hypothetical high school where teachers are working to balance right- and left-hemisphere approaches to their subjects.

The first room is the United States history class. Class is just starting, and as we walk in, the teacher is reading from the letters of a pioneer woman settling in Kansas. It's easy to tell that the class is studying westward expansion because the walls are covered with prints of paintings of the West and copies of photographs from around the 1850s. On the bulletin board geographic maps done by students include the territory of Indian tribes, migration patterns from countries outside the United States, and concentrations of ethnic groups. A time line winds along three sides of the room with entries in a number of colors covering significant events and discoveries in science, technology, politics, and economics.

In one corner is a library of first-person source material (much of it in the form of Xerox copies)—books of diaries, letters, journals—and nonfiction and fiction of and about the period. There are also books that show the fashions, furniture, buildings, and machines of the 1850s. A cassette tape recorder sits on a table nearby with tapes of folk and popular music from that time. The library has been built up over a number of years; some of the materials in it and some of the tapes were made by students in previous classes as part of individual or group projects. Suggestions for projects for this year's class are also in the library.

In the next room is an English class reading *Julius Caesar*. Pictures of ancient Rome (borrowed from the world history teacher) cover one bulletin board. Another is covered with mind maps done in preparation for a written assignment on character development, and a third displays colorful mandalas drawn as part of a book report assignment. Samples of poetry written after a guided fantasy are posted on a free-standing bulletin board. Some poems are illustrated by their authors.

The class is discussing a metaphor assignment of the night before. They were asked to complete the statement: "Antony's friendship was like _____because _____." Now students are offering their metaphors, and a lively discussion goes on about each—"Oh, I thought you meant it was like that because . . . ," "Hey, that could also mean . . . ," "Someone used that metaphor before when we were discussing . . . ," "I think one fits Brutus better because. . . ."

The math class next door is preparing to take an exam. The students are sitting quietly with eyes closed in relaxed postures as the teacher gives them suggestions to calm and center their attention and to help them approach the test in a relaxed and positive manner. Several students sit at a table with manipulatives they will need to use. A couple of students sit separated from each other and from the rest of the class. They need to talk themselves through the problems.

The bulletin boards are covered with exercises that display the spatial and conceptual qualities of mathematics. A large sheet of butcher paper covers one wall. On it are printed several "brain teaser" problems, and written on the paper below and around them are different students' attempts to solve them. The sheet is a visual record of different strategies and approaches at work, and the teacher uses it for regular discussions of how people approach problems. The challenge is not simply to find the solution to a problem but to see how many different ways of solving it are possible.

We can imagine other classrooms in our school—a science class traveling through the digestive system in a guided fantasy, a dance class practicing while blindfolded to direct attention inward, a social studies class involved in a simulation designed to explore decision making. We could walk down the street to an elementary school with classrooms stocked with manipulatives, aquaria, and simple science experiments, with art materials as well as books, with space for movement as well as reading. Out in the community we might encounter an elementary class on a field trip or students from a high school civics course studying their community by becoming actively involved with one of its agencies.

Our walk through the classrooms should not distract us from the fact that the center of all this effort is the mind of the student. The pictures, the music, the stimulating assignments have a common goal—to capture the learner's attention, to present information in a form she can take in, and to encourage her to generate meaning for herself. Learning does not occur in classrooms; it occurs in students' minds. The role of the teacher and the classroom he creates is to offer possibilities in such a way that students will both want and be able to learn. The richer the banquet we lay, the more students will partake and the longer they will stay at the table.

It seems appropriate to close a book on right-hemisphere teaching with a metaphor, and eating offers some interesting parallels to learning. In both cases, an individual must be both *willing* and *able* to take in something (just as some people may want to eat a given food but be unable to digest it, some students struggle to learn but are unable to take in information in the form in which it is offered). Also, in both cases, the individual must act on and process the raw material to convert it into a form in which it can be used. Learners do not passively assimilate meaning; they actively generate it.

As you read these words, your mind is constructing images, making connections, selecting which ideas it considers important. You will remember what you select to remember—those ideas which connect to your experiences and values, which stimulate your imagination, which address your interests and concerns. The process is the same for students. They learn what they choose to learn, and they learn best when they generate meaning *for*

Figure 10.1 (*Author's note:* This mandala was drawn as I struggled to write the final chapter of the book. I knew I needed some way to bring the parts together into a whole. As I drew a mind map, it became clear that a circle was more appropriate; and the mandala developed from there. The writing followed. When I began thinking about this book, the idea of drawing a mandala would not have occurred to me. The mandala is another affirmation of the way that the right hemisphere techniques we use for teaching can enrich our personal lives as well.)

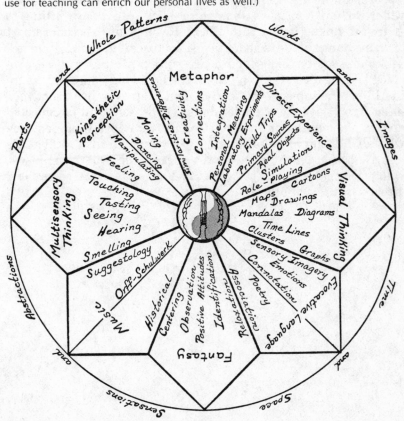

themselves instead of parroting back what they think we want to hear. When we ask them to generate their own metaphors, draw their own diagrams and maps, and create their own mandalas, we not only help them learn the material we're teaching; we allow them to function creatively as active participants in the learning process rather than as passive consumers.

The banquet we spread becomes a potluck feast to which both students and teachers contribute and from which both draw nourishment.

A potluck is a community affair that requires many contributors to be a success. Similarly, teaching is more enjoyable when one can share ideas and efforts. A book, by its nature, is a one-way communication, but this book can become a stimulus to a wider exchange of ideas and energy if its readers are willing to share their experiences with others. If you want to become a part of an exchange of ideas about two-sided teaching, send a stamped, self-addressed envelope and a description of one or more two-sided lessons (preferably typed) to the following address. Be sure to include the subjects you teach and indicate whether or not your name can be sent to other teachers. The lessons will be collected and in six months or so you'll receive the ideas from someone whose work might be of interest to you. You'll also receive the names of other teachers in your area or teachers from other places who teach the same subject and grades so that you can correspond directly with each other.

Two-Sided Teaching
Linda V. Williams
P. O. Box 9563
Berkeley, CA 94709

BIBLIOGRAPHY

Author's Note: This bibliography is not exhaustive, and there are no doubt many fine books that are missing from it. My learning style is primarily auditory; I prefer to learn by watching teachers at work and discussing ideas with them. I read slowly and invest my time only in books I truly love. The weakness of that learning style is apparent when it comes time to prepare a Bibliography. I have compensated by asking people I respect to make some suggestions to supplement my own list. The result, I hope, is a Bibliography that offers a few excellent resources in each area. Its goal is to give you the resources to begin your explorations.

BRAIN RESEARCH

The Brain. San Francisco, Calif.: W. H. Freeman & Company Publishers, 1979. A series of articles from *Scientific American* on the brain, technical but readable, gives a good sense of the complexity of the subject.

Brain-Mind Bulletin. Interface Press, Box 42211, 4717 N. Figueroa St., Los Angeles, CA 90042. A "New Age" newsletter, published every three weeks with information on current research, theory, and practice.

CHALL, JEANNE, and MIRSKY, ALLAN, eds., *Education and the Brain*. Seventy-Seventh Yearbook of the National Society for the Study of Education. Part 2. Chicago: University of Chicago Press, 1978. Articles by experts in neuropsychology and education, an excellent resource for those who want to know more about research on the brain.

GARDINER, HOWARD, *The Shattered Mind*. New York: Knopf, 1975. Information on the brain from studies of brain injured patients, good science and good reading.

MORE, RAYMOND S. and DOROTHY N., et al., *School Can Wait*. Provo, Utah: Brigham Young University Press, 1979. Brings together a great deal of research on the relationship between development and readiness to learn, good chapter on neurophysiology.

ORNSTEIN, ROBERT, *The Psychology of Consciousness*. San Francisco, Calif.: W. H. Freeman & Company Publishers, 1972. The book that introduced a great many people to split-brain research, very readable.

WITTROCK, M. C., ed., *The Human Brain*. Englewood Cliffs, N.J.: Prentice-Hall, 1977. The best nontechnical book on the brain I know of, readable by the layperson but also includes a good discussion of the research, eight chapters, each by a respected scientist, written with educators in mind.

FANTASY

DE MILLE, RICHARD, *Put Your Mother on the Ceiling: Children's Imagination Games*. New York: Penguin, 1973. Wonderful games to introduce children to fantasy.

HENDRICKS, GAY, and FADIMAN, JAMES, *Transpersonal Education: A Curriculum for Feeling and Being*. Englewood Cliffs, N.J.: Prentice-Hall, 1976, pp. 66–76. Articles on guided fantasy and its use in three classrooms.

HENDRICKS, GAY, and ROBERTS, THOMAS B., *The Second Centering Book: More Awareness Activities for Children, Parents, and Teachers*. Englewood Cliffs, N.J.: Prentice-Hall, 1977. More relaxation, centering and fantasy exercises; also communications skills and a section on physical education.

HENDRICKS, GAY, and WILLS, RUSSEL, *The Centering Book: Awareness Activities for Children, Parents, and Teachers*. Englewood Cliffs, N.J.: Prentice-Hall, 1975. A wealth of activities—relaxation, centering, guided imagery, and more.

MALTZ, MAXWELL, *Psycho-Cybernetics*. New York: Simon & Schuster, 1968. An approach using visualization to change behavior and overcome problems.

KINESTHETIC AND MULTISENSORY LEARNING

BOORMAN, JOYCE, *Dance and Language Experiences with Children*. Don Mills, Ont., Canada: Longman Canada Ltd, 1973. Dance activities that provide the basis for exciting language arts lessons.

FURTH, HANS G., and WACHS, HARRY, *Thinking Goes to School: Piaget's Theory in Practice*. New York: Oxford University Press, 1975. Excellent both in theory and practical ideas. A must for all teachers of early elementary, 179 "games" that develop the full range of thinking.

GALLWEY, W. TIMOTHY, *The Inner Game of Tennis*. New York: Random House, 1974. An approach to sports that focuses attention inward.

KOGAN, SHEILA, *Step by Step, A Complete Movement Education Curriculum from Preschool to 6th Grade*. Byron, Calif.: Front Row Experience, 1982 (540 Discovery Bay Blvd., Byron, Calif. 94514). All you need to know about introducing movement into your classroom, including how to generate enthusiasm without chaos.

LEONARD, GEORGE, *The Ultimate Athlete*. New York: Viking, 1975. A new way of looking at athletics and physical activity, inspiring and exciting.

SCHNEIDER, TOM, *Everybody's a Winner*. Boston: Little, Brown, 1976. A Brown Paper School Book, "A Kid's Guide to New Sports and Fitness."

TUTKO, THOMAS and TOSI, UMBERTO, *Sports Psyching: Playing Your Best Game All of the Time*. Los Angeles, Calif.: J. P. Tarcher, 1980. Good discussion of how the mind affects the body's performance and specific directions for "psyching" including imagery rehearsal.

LEARNING DISABILITIES

The books in this section were suggested by Victoria Sperry, a well-known authority in learning disabilities.

HAYES, MARNELL L., *Oh Dear, Somebody Said "Learning Disabilities"!* Novato, Calif.: Academic Therapy Publications, 1975. Practical suggestions for working with children with learning disabilities, includes a set of exercises to help adults experience how it feels to have a disability.

————, *The Tuned-In, Turned-On Book about Learning Problems*. Novato, Calif.: Academic Therapy Publications, 1974. Written for children with learning disabilities by a mother and her twelve-year old daughter, practical strategies for coping, also excellent reading for parents and teachers.

LERNER, JANET W., *Children with Learning Disabilities*, 2nd ed. Boston: Houghton Mifflin Company, 1976. Often used as an introductory text at the college level, a complete and current treatment of the subject.

MARKOFF, ANNABELLE M., *Teaching Low Achieving Children Reading, Spelling, and Handwriting: Developing Perceptual Skills with the Graphic Symbols of the Language*. Springfield, Ill.: Chas. C. Thomas, 1976. The title says it all.

METAPHOR

GORDON, WILLIAM J. J., *Making It Strange, Books I through IV*. New York: Harper & Row, Pub., 1969. Creative writing and thinking for grades three through six, marvelously original.

GORDON, WILLIAM J. J., and POZE, TONY, *From the Inside*.

Cambridge, Mass.: Porpoise Books, 1974. A text for high school and junior college, teaches both creative writing and communication skills.

————, *The Metaphorical Way of Learning and Knowing*. Cambridge, Mass.: Porpoise Books, 1973. The best introduction to metaphorical teaching, includes applications to a variety of subjects and grades, plus counseling; "must reading" for anyone interested in metaphor.

————, *Strange and Familiar, Book III*. Cambridge, Mass.: Porpoise Books, 1975. Connection making in a variety of subjects for elementary students, includes some of the lessons from SES's Title I Project.

————, *Strange and Familiar, Book VI*. Cambridge, Mass.: Porpoise Books, 1972. Connection making for the middle grades, includes lessons in social studies, science, the arts, value clarification, and hypothesis formation; fun even for adults.

————, *Teaching Is Listening*. Cambridge, Mass.: Porpoise Books, 1972. A programmed text designed to train teachers to develop lesson plans based on metaphor.

The books in this section are not available in bookstores. They can be ordered from SES Associates, 121 Brattle Street, Cambridge, MA 02138.

MUSIC—ORFF-SCHULWERK

The books in this section were suggested by Marsha Beck, a well-known authority on Orff-Schulwerk.

American Orff-Schulwerk Association (AOSA), Department of Music, Cleveland State University, Cleveland, OH 44115. A national parent organization offering membership, list of local chapters, convention, and magazine.

Orff Re-Echoes. Cleveland, Ohio: American Orff-Schulwerk Association, 1977. A collection of articles on the Orff-Schulwerk philosophy.

Orff-Schulwerk Music for Children, American ed., Vols. II and III. Mainz, Germany: B. Schott's Sohne, 1980. (Available through Magnamusic Baton, Inc., 10370 Industrial Page Blvd., St. Louis, MO 63132.) Collection of rhymes, games, songs, poetry, etc.

NASH, GRACE, et al., *Do It My Way.* Sherman Oaks, Calif.: Alfred Publishing Co., Inc., 1977. Practical lessons for classroom teachers using songs and chants to teach language arts, math, and other subjects.

MUSIC—SUGGESTOLOGY

OSTRANDER, SHEILA, and SCHROEDER, LYNN, with OSTRANDER, NANCY, *Superlearning.* New York: Delta/Confucian Press, 1980. Description of powerful new learning techniques, including Suggestology and imagery rehearsal.

PRICHARD, ALLYN, and TAYLOR, JEAN, *Accelerating Learning: The Use of Suggestion in the Classroom,* Novato, Calif.: Academic Therapy Publications, 1980. Suggestology techniques applied to an American classroom to teach several different subjects.

PROBLEM SOLVING

ADAMS, JAMES L., *Conceptual Blockbusting: A Guide to Better Ideas,* 2nd ed. New York: W. W. Norton & Co., Inc., 1979. An approach to problem solving that goes beyond verbal, logical thinking to focus on conceptualization and creativity.

BURNS, MARILYN, *The Book of Think or How to Solve a Problem Twice Your Size.* Boston: Little, Brown, 1976. A Brown Paper School Book. Problem solving for kids.

DE BONO, EDWARD, *Lateral Thinking: Creativity Step by Step.* New York: Harper & Row, Pub., 1970. A practical guide to developing nonlinear problem-solving skills, lots of good problems and experiences to practice strategies.

DOYLE, MICHAEL, and STRAUS, DAVID, *How to Make Meetings Work.* Chicago: Playboy Press, 1976. Good practical treatment of group problem solving with the bonus that you can use it to improve your own meetings.

GORDON, WILLIAM J. J., and POZE, TONY, *The Art of the Possible.* Cambridge, Mass.: Porpoise Books, 1976. A programmed text for teaching synectics problem solving to high school students.

————, *The New Art of the Possible.* Cambridge, Mass.: Porpoise Books, 1980. The famous synectics problem-solving method updated and put in the form of a programmed text for adults.

HANKS, KURT, BELLISTON, LARRY, and EDWARDS, DAVE, *Design Yourself.* Los Altos, Calif.: Wm. Kaufman, Inc. An abbreviated version of Hanks and Belliston, *Draw,* with some good information on problem solving.

McKIM, R. H., *Experiences in Visual Thinking.* See "Visual Thinking" section.

STRAUS, DAVID, *Strategy Notebook.* San Francisco, Calif.: Interaction Assoc., 1971. Available from Interaction Associates, 185 Berry St., San Francisco, CA 94107. Identifies and defines thinking strategies, includes exercises using each strategy.

TRANSPERSONAL, AFFECTIVE, AND CONFLUENT EDUCATION

BROWN, GEORGE ISAAC, *Human Teaching for Human Learning: An Introduction to Confluent Education.* New York: Viking, 1971. One of the first books on confluent education: i.e., combining affective and cognitive activities.

CANFIELD, J., and WELLS, H., *100 Ways to Enhance Self-Concept in the Classroom.* Englewood Cliffs, N.J.: Prentice-Hall, 1976. Just what the title says.

HENDRICKS, GAY, and FADIMAN, JAMES, *Transpersonal Education: A Curriculum for Feeling and Being.* Englewood Cliffs, N.J.: Prentice-Hall, 1976. Articles by a number of writers on application of fantasy and other techniques to teaching.

HENDRICKS and ROBERTS, *The Second Centering Book.* See "Fantasy" section.

HENDRICKS and WILLS, *The Centering Book*. See "Fantasy" section.

JONES, RICHARD M., *Fantasy and Feeling in Education*. New York: Harper & Row, Pub., 1978. Uses what we know from psychology to look at what is meaningful to children, an exciting perspective on the learning process.

VISUAL THINKING

ARGUELLES, JOSE and MIRIAM, *Mandala*. Berkeley, Calif.: Shambala, 1972. Beautiful book on mandalas as spiritual tools.

ARNHEIM, RUDOLF, *Visual Thinking*. Berkeley, Calif.: University of California Press, 1971. Classic book on the relation of vision to thinking and to art.

BUCKLEY, MARILYN HANF, and BOYLE, OWEN, *Mapping the Writing Journey*. Berkeley, Calif.: Bay Area Writing Project, 1981 (5635 Tolman Hall, University of California, Berkeley, CA 94720). An excellent discussion of mapping and its use in writing, includes examples of student work.

BUZAN, TONY, *Use Both Sides of Your Brain*. New York: Dutton, 1974. New techniques for studying, reading, remembering, and problem solving; a good section on mapping.

EDWARDS, BETTY, *Drawing on the Right Side of the Brain*. Los Angeles, Calif.: J. P. Tarcher, 1979. Exciting approach to learning to draw using the right-left brain model.

HANKS, KURT, and BELLISTON, LARRY, *Draw*. Los Altos, Calif.: Wm. Kaufman, Inc., 1977. Presents "drawing used as a tool for Ideation, Understanding, and Communication" (p. 145), includes many good examples of graphic representation.

McKIM, R. H., *Experiences in Visual Thinking*. Monterey, Calif.: Brooks/Cole, 1972. Excellent discussion of visual thinking and strategies along with exercises for developing one's own visual capacities; my choice for the best book on visual thinking.

Neuro-Linguistic Programming in Education. Santa Cruz, Calif.: Not Ltd Division of Training and Research, 1980 (517 Mission St., Santa Cruz, CA 95060). A booklet on the application of Neuro-Linguistic Programming theory to education, includes directions for the NLP approach to spelling.

NICOLAIDES, KIMON, *The Natural Way to Draw*. Boston: Houghton Mifflin Company, 1941. A series of exercises designed to help you teach yourself to draw, a classic in the field.

O'NEILL, DAN, MARIAN and HUGH JR., *The Big Yellow Drawing Book*. Nevada City, Calif.: Hugh O'Neill and Associates, 1974. Available from Hugh O'Neill and Associates, Box 1297, Nevada City, CA 95959. An excellent introduction to both cartooning and drawing, a perfect place to start for those who feel insecure about their drawing ability.

PARMENTER, ROSS, *The Awakened Eye*. Middletown, Conn.: Wesleyan University Press, 1968. A discussion of visual perception based on the author's experience.

PRESSLEY, MARJORIE, et al., *The Mind's Eye*. Escondido, Calif.: Escondido Union School District Board of Education, 1979. Excellent curriculum for using visualization to improve reading comprehension.

RICO, GABRIELE LUSSER, and CLAGGETT, MARY FRANCES, *Balancing the Hemispheres: Brain Research and the Teaching of Writing*. Berkeley, Calif.: Bay Area Writing Project, 1980 (5635 Tolman Hall, University of California, Berkeley, CA 94720). An excellent book on using visual strategies to teach writing, thorough directions for using mapping and mandalas plus examples of student work.

WALBERG, FRANETTE, *Puzzle Thinking*. Philadelphia, Penn.: The Franklin Institute Press, 1980. A beautifully thought out approach to teaching math problem solving and logic, uses visual strategies well.

CURRICULUM MATERIALS: LANGUAGE ARTS

BOORMAN, *Dance and Language Experiences with Children*. See "Kinesthetic and Multisensory Learning."

BUCKLEY and BOYLE, *Mapping the Writing Journey*. See "Visual Thinking."

GORDON, *From the Inside.* See "Metaphor."

GORDON and POZE, *Making It Strange, Books I through IV.* See "Metaphor."

GORDON and POZE, *Strange and Familiar, Books III and VI.* See "Metaphor."

KOHL, HERBERT R., *Math and Writing Games in the Open Classroom.* New York: A New York Review Book, 1974. How to make games a vital part of the learning process.

MOFFETT, JAMES, and WAGNER, BETTY JANE, *Student Centered Language Arts and Reading, K–13: A Handbook for Teachers,* 2nd ed. Boston: Houghton Mifflin Company, 1976. Recommended reading for any teacher of language arts—excellent practical ideas but also a wise, holistic sense of the subject.

Neuro-Linguistic Programming in Education. See "Visual Thinking."

PRESSLEY et al., *The Mind's Eye.* See "Visual Thinking."

RICO and CLAGGETT, *Balancing the Hemispheres: Brain Research and the Teaching of Writing.* See "Visual Thinking."

CURRICULUM MATERIALS: MATH

BARATTA-LORTON, MARY, *Math Their Way.* Reading, Mass.: Addison-Wesley, 1976. See description under *Math Manipulatives* in Chapter 7.

BURNS, MARILYN, *The I Hate Mathematics! Book.* Boston: Little, Brown, 1975. A Brown Paper School Book. Written for kids to "turn them on" to the subject in a new way.

Creative Publications, 1101 San Antonio Rd., Mountain View, CA 94043. These folks produce a wealth of good math materials; send for a catalog.

Cuisenaire Company of America, Inc., 12 Church St., New Rochelle, NY 10805. Another excellent source of materials.

DAVIDSON, PATRICIA S., and MAROLDA, MARIA, *Mathematics Diagnostic/Prescriptive Inventory (MDPI).* In preparation. An individualized test designed to assess achievement, ability, and learning style in mathematics.

JACOBS, HAROLD, *Mathematics, A Human Endeavor: A Textbook for Those Who Think They Don't Like the Subject.* San Francisco, Calif.: W. J. Freeman, 1970. An excellent book for grades 6–12.

KOHL, HERBERT R., *Math and Writing Games in the Open Classroom.* See "Curriculum Materials: Language Arts."

LIEBERTHAL, EDWIN, and GURAU, PETER, *The Complete Book of Fingermath.* New York: McGraw-Hill, 1979. "All you need to know to master the fingermath method."

LOVIGLIO, LORRAINE, "Mathematics and the Brain: A Tale of Two Hemispheres," *The Massachusetts Teacher* (January–February 1981). Discusses Patricia Davidson's work on math learning styles.

WALBERG, *Puzzle Thinking.* See "Visual Thinking."

CURRICULUM MATERIALS: SCIENCE

Brown Paper School Books, Boston: Little, Brown and Company. This is an excellent series of books written for kids and grownups together. They use simple, easily available materials to explore science and other subjects and encourage learning by doing.

ALLISON, LINDA, *Blood and Guts: A Working Guide to Your Own Insides* (1976).

———, *The Reasons for Seasons: The Great Cosmic Megagalactic Trip Without Moving Your Chair* (1975).

BURNS, MARILYN, *Good for Me!: All About Food in 32 Bites* (1978).

———, *This Book Is About Time* (1978).

JOBB, JAMIE, *The Night Sky Book: An Everyday Guide to Every Night* (1977).

RIGHTS, MOLLIE, *Beastly Neighbors: All About Wild Things in the City or Why Earwigs Make Good Mothers* (1981).

COBB, VICKI, *Science Experiments You can Eat.* Philadelphia, Penn.: Lippincott, 1972. Science in the kitchen.

SCIIS (Science Curriculum Improvement Study), Delta Education, Box M, Nashua, NH 03061. Superb. Described in Chapter 7.

INDEX

Abacus, 153
Abstract visual imagery, 42
Affirmation, 161–62
Aikido, 160
Alexeyev, Vasily, 160
Analogical thinking (*see* Metaphor)
Architecture, field trips and, 173
Aristotle, 80
Art, 51
   fantasy and, 132
   other subjects and, 105–6
   perception and, 87, 88–89
   time lines and, 96–97
   in Waldorf schools, 106–7
Auditory learning style , 48–49
Auditory processing, 145 (*see also*
   Music)

Backiel, Mitch, 177
Balancing the Hemispheres (Rico and
   Claggett), 101
Baratta-Lorton, Mary, 153
Big Yellow Drawing Book, The
   (O'Neills), 103
Biology:
   field trips and, 173
   simulation and, 177

Bogen, Joseph E., 19
Boorman, Joyce, 154
Boyle, Owen, 100
Brain injured patients, 15–16, 20
Broca, Paul, 15
Brown Paper School series, 171
Buckley, Marilyn Hanf, 100
Burns, Robert, 33, 74–75
Buzan, Tony, 98–99

Cartooning, 93, 101, 103
Change, planning for, 182–84
Charts, 47, 93, 94–95
Chemistry, smell and, 162
Civics courses, 96–97, 101, 177
Claggett, Mary Frances, 97, 98, 101,
   107
Clustering, 94, 98, 99
Collages, 106
Color, 107–8
Commissurotomy, 17–19
Concentration, 139
Connection-making process (see
   Metaphor)
Constructions, 105, 106
Coordination, 149–50
Corpus callosum, 17

Creativity, 5–7
  metaphor and, 72–74

Dance, 154–55
*Dance and Language Experiences with
  Children* (Boorman), 154
Davidson, Patricia, 9, 27, 29–30, 153
Davis, Gene, 70, 103, 112
Diagrams, 93, 94–96
Dichotic listening, 21, 24
Direct experience, 11, 34–35, 40–52,
  169–79
  field trips, 170, 172–73
  laboratory experiments, 170–72
  primary sources, 35, 170, 174–75
  real objects, 35, 170, 173–74
  role playing, 35, 170, 175, 177–79
  simulation, 35, 170, 175–77
Drawing, 86, 88–89
  as approach to problem solving, 42,
    43–45, 47
  expressive, 105–7
*Drawing on the Right Side of the
  Brain* (Edwards), 87
Dyslexia, 28

Edison, Thomas, 149
Edwards, Betty, 87
Einstein, Albert, 31, 117, 149
Elementary education:
  art activities, 105–6
  field trips, 172–73
  laboratory experiments, 171
  metaphor and, 75–78
  sensory learning in, 146–49
English (*see* Literature; Reading;
  Spelling; Vocabulary; Writing)
Epilepsy, 17
Evaluation, metaphors and, 78–80
Evocative language, 32–33
Expectations, 185, 186
Experiential learning (*see* Direct
  experience)
Expressive drawings, 105–7

Family histories, 174–75
Fantasy, 11, 32, 74–75, 108, 116–41
  as basis for self-expression, 132–34
  evaluating products of, 134–35
  experiencing, 119–24
  grammar and, 8–9

history and, 127, 129–31
  identification, 122–24, 126–32
  math and, 123
  observation, 121–22, 124–26
  relaxation and, 121, 136
  as review technique, 124–25
  study habits and, 139–40
  use of in classroom, 135–38
  writing and, 125–26, 132–34
Field trips, 170, 172–73
Films, 91
Finger math, 153
Foreign language:
  gesture and, 155–56
  music education and, 35, 164–65
Frostig, Marianne, 186
Furth, Hans G., 148, 149–50

Galyean, Beverly, 138–39
Gender, 25
Geography, fantasy and, 123
Geometry, fantasy and, 123
Gesture, 155–56
Gordon, William J. J., 128
Grading writing assignments, 134–35
Grammar, fantasy and, 8–9, 117
Graphic representation, 86, 92–108
  cartoons, 93, 101, 103
  charts, diagrams, and graphs, 93,
    94–96
  color, 107–8
  constructions, 105, 106
  expressive drawings, 105–7
  idea sketches, 93, 104–5
  key words, 93–94
  mandalas, 93, 101, 102
  mapping, 93, 97–100
  time lines, 96–97
Graphs, 93, 94
Greeks, ancient, 14
Griffith, Coleman R., 157
Grishaver, Alex, 111

Hawthorne, Trish, 173
History, 192–93
  drawing in, 105, 106
  fantasy and, 127, 129–31
  field trips and, 173
  idea sketches and, 105
  memorization, 111
  metaphor and, 64–65, 69–71, 75

music education and, 164
perception and, 90
primary sources and, 174–75
time lines and, 96

Idea sketches, 93, 104–5
Identification fantasies, 122–24,
126–32
Imagery rehearsal, 160–62
Insight, 5–6
Intangibles in teaching, 185–87
Ipsen, Zoc, 171

Jones, Ron, 177

Kaplan, Edith, 20
Kellogg, Rhoda, 101
Key words in graphic representation,
93–94
Kinesthetic learning, 11, 42, 44,
48–49, 127, 144, 145, 150–62
Kogan, Sheila, 154

Labels, 124
Laboratory experiments, 170–72
Lane, John, 111
Language, 23–24, 26
Language arts (*see* Literature; Read-
ing; Spelling; Vocabulary;
Writing)
Laucirica, Aleida, 155
Learning disabilities, 27–28, 185, 189
sensory-motor integration and,
149–50
smell and taste and, 163
Learning styles, 48–50
Lectures, 7, 8, 33, 111, 168
Left-hemisphere of brain:
differences between right and,
18–25
injury to, 15
processing, 2–5, 22–27
Levin, Joel R., 109
Levy, Jerre, 22
Linear processing, 2–3, 97, 98
Listening skills, 68
Literature, 193
mandalas and, 101
metaphor and, 74
role playing and, 177–79
"Loci" method, 110–11

Logical thinking, 5, 6
Logic problems, 46
Lower-class children, 77
Lozanov, Georgi, 35, 165–66

McKim, Robert, 89–90, 93, 152
Mandalas, 93, 101, 102, 195
Mapping, 93, 97–100
Maslow, Phyllis, 186
Math, 75, 193–94
charts and graphs, 94, 95–96
color, use of, 107
fantasy and, 123
kinesthetic learning and, 152–54
learning styles in, 9, 27, 29–30
music education and, 164
perception and, 85
simulation and, 176
visualization and, 86
Mathematical approach to problem
solving, 42, 44, 45
Math Their Way (Baratta-Lorton), 153
Memory, 65, 109–11
gesture and, 155
music education and, 163
Mental imagery (*see* Visualization)
Mental set, 160
Metaphor, 6, 11, 33–34, 55–82, 194
advantages of teaching through,
58–61
common problems with use of,
65–66
evaluation of, 78–80
generating, 61–63, 66–68
history and, 64–65, 69–71, 75
integrating different subjects,
75–76
introducing material, 68–70
literature and, 74
science and, 33–34, 56, 60–64,
69–70, 75
setting content goals, 63–65
structuring, clarifying, and reviewing, 70–71
testing and, 71–72
writing and, 72–74
Microcomputers, 10
Miller, Genie, 106
Mind mapping, 94, 98–99
"Mind's Eye" project, The, 109
Minority children, 77

Moby Dick (Melville), 74
Motivation, 185, 186–87
Movement games, 154
Multisensory learning, 11, 35, 144–66
  in early primary grades, 146–49
  kinesthetic system, 144, 145,
    150–62
  sensory-motor integration, 146,
    149–50
  smell and taste, 162–63
  tactile learning, 150–52
Musante, Marjorie, 172, 176
Music, 11, 35, 75, 163–66
  fantasy and, 132
  kinesthetic learning and, 157
  perception of, 26, 27
"My Love Is Like a Red, Red Rose"
  (Burns), 75

Name-shape dichotomy, 22
Negative imagination, 138
Neuro-Linguistic Programming
  (NLP), 112
Nicolaides, Kimon, 89

Objective language, 32–33
Observation, 85, 86–92
Observation fantasies, 121–22,
  124–26
O'Neill, Dan, 103
O'Neill, Hugh, Jr., 103
O'Neill, Marian, 103
Orff-Schulwerk philosophy of music
  education, 155, 163–64
Outlining, 97

Parallel (holistic) processing,
  22–23, 26
Parmenter, Ross, 88, 90
Patterson, Janet, 125
Perception, 85, 86–92
Percival, Lloyd, 157
Philosophy, time lines and, 96–97
Photo essays, 91
Physical education:
  fantasy and, 132
  kinesthetic learning and, 156–61
  perception and, 87
Piaget, Jean, 148
Poetry, metaphor and, 74–75
Politics, time lines and, 96–97

Poze, Tony, 128
Primary source material, 35, 170,
  174–75
Problem-solving style, 7, 40–52
Process awareness, 50–52
Puzzle Thinking (Walberg), 95

Reading:
  comprehension, 108–9
  fantasy and, 123
  sensory-motor integration and, 147
  simulation and, 176
Real objects, 35, 170, 173–74
Relativity, theory of, 117
Relaxation, 112, 160, 193
  fantasy and, 121, 136
Religion, time lines and, 96–97
Review technique, fantasy as, 124–25
Rice, Anne, 74
Rico, Gabriele, 98, 101
Right-handers, 15, 19
Right-hemisphere of brain:
  differences between left and, 18–25
  injury to, 15–16
  processing, 2–5, 22–27, 56–57
Rodin, Auguste, 149
Role playing, 35, 170, 175, 177–79

Science, 7–8, 31, 51
  charts and graphs, 94
  field trips, 173
  idea sketches, 105
  laboratory experiments, 171
  metaphor and, 33–34, 56, 60–64,
    69–70, 75
  perception, 85, 86
  simulation, 176
  smell and, 162
  time lines and, 96–97
SCIIS (Science Curriculum Improvement Study), 148, 171
Self-expression, fantasy as basis for,
  132–34
Sensory-motor integration, 146,
  149–50
Sensory systems, learning styles and,
  49–50
Sequential processing, 2–5, 22–23,
  25–26
Serial processing, 22–23
Sewing:

fantasy and, 132
  kinesthetic learning and, 157
Shakespeare, William, 74
Shop, kinesthetic learning and, 157
Simonides, 110
Simulation, 35, 170, 175–77
Simultaneous processing, 4, 5, 22–23, 26
Smell, 162–63
Social studies, 68
  drawing and, 105
  perception and, 86, 90
  simulation, 176
Sonnet XVIII (Shakespeare), 74
Speech, 15, 23–24
Spelling, 49, 112
  music education and, 164
  simulation, 176
  visualization, 86
Sperry, Roger, 16–17
Split-brain surgery, 17–20, 22, 24
Step by Step (Kogan), 154
Stovel, Jack, 69
Strategies for problem solving, 47–50
Streeter, Diane, 8–9
"Stretching exercise," 73–74
Study habits, fantasy and, 139–40
Suggestology, 155–56, 165–66
Support groups, 189
Synectics Education Systems (SES), 68, 72, 73, 75–77

Tachistoscope, 21
Tactile learning, 16, 25, 150–52
Taste, 162–63
Teaching Is Listening (Gordon and Poze), 128
Technology, time lines and, 96–97
Testing:
  metaphor and, 71–72
  visualization and, 112
Textbooks, 7, 168
Time lines, 96–97
Total communication approach, 155
Trevarthen, Colwyn, 22
Trust, 78, 134, 185, 186
Typing, kinesthetic learning and, 157, 159

Use Both Sides of Your Brain
  (Buzan), 98–99

Verbal description, 89–92
Verbal instruction in kinesthetic
  learning, 158–59
Verbal problem solving, 43–45
Vestibular system, 144–45
Villalon, Anne, 106
Visceral system, 144, 145
Visualization, 11, 30–32, 42–45,
  47–49, 52, 85–113, 145
  math and, 86
  memory, 109–11
  reading comprehension, 108–9
  spelling, 112
  testing, 112
Visual thinking (*see* Graphic repre-
  sentation; Perception;
  Visualization)
Visuo-spatial tasks, 18–20, 26–27
Vocabulary, 31
  movement and, 155
  simulation and, 176
Vocational education, 35, 85, 87

Wach, Harry, 148, 149–50
Walberg, Franette, 95
Waldorf schools, 106
Wernicke, Carl, 15
Williams, Andrew, 95
Wittrock, M. C., 31
Working backward, 47
Woulf, Connie, 177–78
Writing, 51, 75
  art and, 105–6
  clustering, 98–99
  color, use of, 107
  fantasy and, 125–26, 132–34
  grading, 134–35
  idea sketches, 105
  metaphor and, 72–74
  movement and, 155
  perception and, 90, 92
  simulation and, 176
  time lines and, 97